The Home

SOUTHAMPTON INSTITUTE

The Home

Its Work and Influence

CHARLOTTE PERKINS GILMAN

A REPRINT OF THE 1903 EDITION
WITH AN INTRODUCTION BY
MICHAEL KIMMEL

ALTAMIRA
PRESS
A Division of
ROWMAN & LITTLEFIELD PUBLISHERS, INC.
Walnut Creek • Lanham • New York • Oxford

ALTAMIRA PRESS
A Division of Rowman & Littlefield Publishers, Inc.
1630 North Main Street, #367
Walnut Creek, CA 94596
www.altamirapress.com

Rowman & Littlefield Publishers, Inc.
4720 Boston Way
Lanham, MD 20706

PO Box 317
Oxford
OX2 9RU, UK

British Library Cataloguing in Publication Information Available

Library of Congress Cataloging-in-Publication Data

Gilman, Charlotte Perkins, 1860–1935.
   The home, its work and influence / Charlotte Perkins Gilman.—A reprint of the 1903
ed. / with an introduction by Michael Kimmel.
      p. cm.—(Classics in gender studies)
   Originally published: New York : McClure, Phillips, 1903.
   Includes bibliographical references.
   ISBN 0-7591-0305-4 (cloth : alk. paper)
   1. Home. I. Title. II. Series.

HQ734 .G5 2002
640—dc21

                                                                          2002066632

Printed in the United States of America
⊖™ The paper used in this publication meets the minimum requirements of American
National Standard for Information Sciences—Permanence of Paper for Printed Library
Materials, ANSI/NISO Z39.48–1992.

CLASSICS IN GENDER STUDIES

Series Editor
Michael Kimmel
Dept. of Sociology
SUNY at Stony Brook
Stony Brook, NY 11794

Each generation of scholars rediscovers the "classics" that it needs. These works ground our contemporary research and provide historical context. What makes them "classics" is not simply that they're old, but that they continue to speak to contemporary concerns. Sadly, many brilliant works by major scholars and thinkers that were so influential in their time have passed out of print. The books in this series will reintroduce these works both to established scholars and to a new generation of students and researchers as they examine the origins of our understanding of contemporary gender relations.

BOOKS IN THE SERIES

The Home: Its Work and Influence, Charlotte Perkins Gilman (2002)
Reprint of the 1903 edition with an introduction by Michael Kimmel

Classics in Gender Studies Series
AltaMira Press
1630 North Main Street #367
Walnut Creek, CA 94596
(925) 938-7243
www.altamirapress.com

INTRODUCTION TO THE
ALTAMIRA PRESS EDITION

FORTY years ago, Betty Friedan shattered the silence that surrounded the "feminine mystique," the ideology that traps the American woman into a mind-numbing and self-stultifying routine. "Her day is fragmented as she rushes from dishwasher to washing machine to telephone to dryer to station wagon to supermarket, and delivers Johnny to the Little League field, takes Janey to dancing class, gets the lawnmower fixed and meets the 6:45." Bored and depressed, she wanders through her life without ever inhabiting the space she occupies, never really claiming a self. She's less constrained physically than mentally; "The chains that bind her in her trap are chains in her own mind and spirit." Thus, Friedan argued, women must break the chains that bind them to the feminine mystique, escape the prison of their homes, and enter the wide world of work, of public life—indeed, of life itself.[1]

---

[1] Betty Friedan, *The Feminine Mystique*. [1963]. New York: Dell, 1983, p. 30.

INTRODUCTION

Her message resounded across America like an alarm clock, waking women from an ideologically induced slumber. And her anger resonated with the rumblings of women all over the world for a life less circumscribed by laundry lists and dishwashing. More than any other single text, *The Feminine Mystique* was hailed as the bible of the modern women's movement, its touchstone foundational text.

We often forget that sixty years earlier, 100 years ago, an American feminist issued a similar and equally powerful indictment of domestic life. Charlotte Perkins Gilman's *The Home* (1903) sounded a similar alarm and offered a program of domestic reform that inspired women at the beginning of what became a century-long struggle. Sixty years before Friedan coined the term "the feminine mystique," Gilman was already tearing down the walls of women's "arbitrary imprisonment." And, like Friedan, Gilman argued that such "exclusive confinement" in the home made the woman less of a person; a "mental myopia" comes over her as she focuses only on the proximate, to the exclusion of the visionary.[2]

Gilman was already a well-known writer and thinker by the time she published *The Home*. Her breakthrough work, *Women and Economics* (1898) was a bestseller, and cata-

---

[2] Charlotte Perkins Gilman, *The Home* (New York: McClure, Phillips and Co., 1903), pp. 22, 23, 216.

pulted Gilman into the prestigious ranks of public intellectuals—one whose works were as respected among scholars as they were influential among a larger public.

She was born Charlotte Anna Perkins on July 3, 1860, in Hartford, Connecticut to one of the nineteenth century's most prominent families. Charlotte's father was a ne'er do well and a dilettante. He attended Yale but never graduated, studied law but never practiced, and abandoned the family soon after Charlotte's birth, returning only for occasional visits before the couple formally divorced in 1873. Never particularly feminine—she was physically strong, vigorous, and was passionate about sports—Charlotte first thought to be an artist, and entered the newly opened Rhode Island School of Design in 1878. Family problems intervened and she left school without graduating; her early training, however, provided her with the basis to earn a living as a commercial artist.

Early in 1882, she met Charles Walter Stetson, a promising young artist in Providence. Their courtship was difficult and turbulent. Charlotte had resolved to remain single and devote herself to her career. Eventually, she capitulated to Walter's earnest courtship, and they were married in May 1884.

But Charlotte felt constantly torn. Marriage was a life or death struggle for women, tearing them between two irreconcilable passions—motherhood and career.[3] Charles may have been attentive, dutiful and even helped with the housework, but it could not resolve the tensions Charlotte felt, especially after the birth of her daughter, Katherine in March 1885. At first Charlotte was overjoyed by motherhood, but she gradually sank into what she described as a "growing melancholia," a "constant dragging weariness miles below zero."[4]

Her emotional distress became increasingly acute. By 1887, Charlotte's depression had become so serious and debilitating that she sought the advice of Dr. S. Weir Mitchell, the Philadelphia physician who had gained national fame for his treatment of a somewhat trendy, elite condition called "neurasthenia." Mitchell saw neurasthenia—a nervous disorder marked by both anxiety and depression—as a consequence of the over-civilized modern life, "that of the business man exhausted from too much work, and the society woman exhausted from too much play," as Charlotte described it.[5] In both cases, neurasthenia was marked by gender nonconformity. For men, that meant passivity and

---

[3] See, for example, "On Advertising for Marriage" in *Alpha*, vol. 2, and "The Answer" in *Woman's Journal*, volume XVII, Number 40, October 2, 1886.

[4] *The Living* . . . p. 90, 91.

[5] *The Living* . . . p. 95.

lassitude, derived from the sedentary effects of the modern workplace; for women, by contrast, neurasthenia was marked by depression over the balance between work and family, and the inability to function as properly feminine.

Mitchell's remedies returned to traditional gender norms and a strict separation of spheres. Mitchell told Charlotte to "Live as domestic a life as possible. Have your child with you all the time. Lie down an hour after each meal. Have but two hours intellectual life a day. And never touch a pen, brush, or pencil as long as you live." She tried. She "went home, followed those directions rigidly for months, and came perilously close to losing my mind."[6]

So, one day, Charlotte got out of bed, took her daughter, and left her husband, traveling first to Pasadena and then to Oakland, California to live with her best friend, Grace Channing. Her diary entry reads: "Thirty years old. Made a wrong marriage—lots of people do. Am heavily damaged but not dead."

In California, Charlotte threw herself into work, and established her lifelong career as a writer and editor. Between 1888, when she left Walter Stetson, to her death in 1935, Gilman published 8 novels, 171 short stories, 473 poems,

---

[6] *The Living* . . . p. 96.

INTRODUCTION

and 1,472 nonfiction pieces—9 of them books.[7] In her *Forerunner* magazine alone, she wrote critical articles, editorials, essays, poetry, reviews, short fiction, and two serialized books a year; the full seven-year run of the magazine equaled some 28 full-length books.[8] Yet prolific as she was, Gilman's writing turned on a few dominant themes: the transformation of marriage, the family, and the home.

And even these returned insistently to her central argument, that "the economic independence and specialization of women as essential to the improvement of marriage, motherhood, domestic industry, and racial improvement."[9] The liberation of women—and of children and of men, for that matter—required getting women out of the house, both practically and ideologically. It was work that was "the normal life of every human being; work, which is joy and growth and service, without which one is a pauper and a parasite."

In 1898, Charlotte published *Women and Economics*, her breakthrough work of nonfiction, and perhaps her single greatest book. Subtitled "A Study of the Economic Relations between Men and Women as a Factor in Social Evolu-

---

[7] Gary Scharnhorst, *Charlotte Perkins Gilman: A Bibliography* (Metuchen, NJ: Scarecrow Press, 1985).

[8] *Herland*, Ann Lane, ed. (New York: Pantheon, 1979), vi.

[9] *The Living* . . . p. 186.

tion," the book was an immediate success, widely read and discussed both in the United States and abroad. The book, which *The Nation* called "the most significant utterance on the subject of women since Mill's *The Subjection of Women*," established Charlotte as the leading intellectual in the American women's movement.

In this work, Gilman drew from several different sources to produce a groundbreaking and original synthesis. From Marx and others, she took the idea that the central arena of human life is the realm of production, and that the workplace was the site of both oppression and liberation. What's more, she also agreed that the differences among people were not to be found in nature, in biological differences, but rather from the way they are raised.[10] But unlike Marx, who had limited his discussion to economic classes, Gilman applied the idea to gender. Women and men are far more alike than they are different, she argued, but they are socialized to be dramatically different and at a cost to both women and men. From Darwin, she took the idea of progress and evolution. We have changed, she observed, and

---

[10] As in Marx's famous epigram that "men make their own history," was echoed in his most famous articulation of this social constructionist position, in the Preface to his 1859 *Contribution to the Critique of Political Economy*, where he writes that "it is not the consciousness of men that determines their being, but, on the contrary, their being which determines their consciousness."

thus we can change and we must change. A theory of evolution underlies all Gilman's work, from her critique of the home as an anachronistic throwback to her vision of a future of economic independence and professional housework and child-care. From Thorstein Veblen she took the blistering critique of woman as ornament, as a medium of exchange between men. And from the sociologist Lester Ward she took the idea that women, not men, were the originators of evolution, the origin of the species. Ward was, Gilman wrote, "quite the greatest man I have ever known" and his "gyneco-centric" theory she thought "the greatest single contribution to the world's thought since Evolution."[11]

In *Women and Economics*, she foreshadowed many of the themes she raised five years later in *The Home*. But if the former work explained the history of woman's imprisonment and the promise of her liberation, it was in *The Home* that she gave her analysis of women's socially produced incapacity its fullest treatment. It was the book that Gilman herself called "the most heretical—and the most amusing—of anything I've done."[12]

Gilman argues that the separation of spheres was both temporal and spatial. While the public arena changes at a dizzying speed, propelled by technological and economic

---

[11] *The Living* . . . p. 187.
[12] *The Living* . . . p. 286.

forces, the domestic domain remains static, timeless. The home "has not developed in proportion to our other institutions, and by its rudimentary condition it arrests development . . ."[13] An evolutionary throwback, the ideal of the home was derived from an earlier time. It is a living anachronism.

And as such it freezes women in that static, airless place. Women are not this way to begin with—their incapacity is produced by these perverse spatial arrangements. "It is not that women are really smaller-minded, weaker-minded, more timid and vacillating," she writes, "but that whosoever, man or woman, lives always in a small dark place, is always guarded, protected, directed and restrained, will become inevitably narrowed and weakened by it. The woman is narrowed by the home and the man is narrowed by the woman."[14]

This makes the woman far less attractive to her husband than misty ideology might suggest. "We are taught that man most loves and admires the domestic type of woman," she writes. "This is one of the roaring jokes of history. The breakers of hearts, the queens of romance, the goddesses of a thousand devotees, have not been cooks." In fact, she ar-

---

[13] *The Home*, p. 10.
[14] *The Home*, p. 129.

gues, if a man loves his wife, "it is in spite of the home—not because of it."[15]

The present arrangement works emotionally best for the man—but only because, as Gilman writes "he is least in it." The woman believes that by sheer force of her love, she can make things right, that "her love for her family makes her service satisfactory." This is not healthy for wives, husbands, or children.[16]

Not only does the current organization of the home make little emotional sense, it makes virtually no economic sense. The individual woman is expected to be a master of a "swarming heap of rudimentary trades." But why? We don't expect each person to make his or her own shoes, do we? Then why would we expect everyone to cook their own meals? Think of it this way, she writes in an article a year later:

We take half the people of the world and set them to wait upon the other half, thus limiting the output of their labor exactly as it would that of a lumber camp if half the men were assigned to wait upon the other half instead of chopping wood; or of an army if half the soldiers were 'keeping

---

[15] *The Home*, p. 280, 281.
[16] *The Home*, p. 73, 100

tent' instead of fighting; or of a ship's crew if half the sailors were cooks.[17]

She calculates that the traditional nuclear family—with working husband and a full-time domesticated wife—is three times more costly than what is necessary to meet the same needs. What waste! And who can afford it?

If women worked outside the home, she calculates, the husband would be "relieved of two-thirds of his expenses; provided with double supplies; properly fed and more comfortable at home than he ever dreamed of being, and associated with a strong, free, stimulating companion all through life, will be able to work to far better purpose in the social service, and with far greater power, pride, and enjoyment."[18]

Her solutions are simple: liberate women to work outside the home, and professionalize those household tasks to which she is currently chained. This doesn't necessarily require the assembly of a large household staff to fulfill all household tasks; rather, she suggests, these could be socialized so that one professional could do all the child-care, or cooking, or laundry, for a group of families. Each family would then contribute only a fraction of the additional in-

---

[17] Charlotte Perkins Gilman, "Domestic Economy" in *The Independent*, June 16, 1904, p. 1161.

[18] *The Home*, p. 320, 322.

come they would be accumulating by enabling the wife to work.

She gives little thought to a reversal of roles. "Never was any such idiot on earth as this hypothetical home-husband. It was not in him to stay in such primitive restrictions. But he has been quite willing to leave his wife in that interestingly remote period."[19] Rather, she believes in equal partnership—equal outside the home and equal within it.

Gilman believes fervently that only by freeing women from the home can they be happy. But more than that, it is also the only way for *men* to be happy—to be happily married to women who are interesting, alive, and engaged with the world around them. Listen to how contemporary, how prescient, are Gilman's words from an essay in 1906:

> We have so arranged life that a man may have a home and family, love, companionship, domesticity, and fatherhood, yet remain an active citizen of age and country. We have so arranged life, on the other hand, that a woman must 'choose'; must either live alone, unloved, uncompanied, uncared for, homeless, childless, with her work in the world for sole consolation; or give up all world-service for the joys of love, motherhood, and domestic service.[20]

---

[19] *The Home*, p. 100.

[20] Charlotte Perkins Gilman, "Passing of Matrimony" in *Harper's Bazaar*, June, 1906, p. 496.

INTRODUCTION

As she winds her way through the history and contemporary consequences of the separation of spheres, Gilman often pauses, and tosses out a small, undigested nugget, the implications of which she barely grasps, and occasionally one with which we are yet to grapple as well. For example, she notes that "the poorer people are, the more they pay for food," a simple empirical truth that still manages to elude contemporary conservative policy-makers.[21]

In this book, Gilman also raises a new issue, one to which she will return in later works, especially her fiction: violence against women. Though she was not the first to explore the question of domestic violence or marital rape, her emphasis that the origins of such abuses were not to be found in demented, perverse, or evil individuals, or in "demon rum," but in the structure of the arrangements between women and men, and especially in women's economic dependence on men, were astonishingly new, and would resound across the twentieth century as women became increasingly aware of the severity and the extent of violence.

Here, she barely raises the issue. Women, current ideology holds, "must be guarded in the only place of safety,

---

[21] *The Home*, p. 132

the home." But, she asks, "[g]uarded from what? From men. From the womanless men who may be prowling about while all women stay at home. The home is safe because women are there. Out of doors is unsafe because women are not there. If women were there, everywhere, in the world which belongs to them as much as to men, then everywhere would be safe."[22]

At the end of one chapter, Gilman writes an apt summary of her argument: "Our present home is injured by the rigidly enforced maintenance of long-outgrown conditions," she writes. "We may free ourselves, if we will, from every one of those injurious, old conditions, and still retain all that is good and beautiful and right in the home."[23] Only by reuniting the separate spheres can women and men—and their children—become full, whole, and happy individuals. Our struggle to feel at home in the world is complemented by an equally important struggle to feel the presence of the world inside our homes.

---

[22] *The Home*, p. 254.
[23] *The Home*, p. 81.

CONTENTS

I

INTRODUCTORY

IN offering this study to a public accustomed only to the unquestioning acceptance of the home as something perfect, holy, quite above discussion, a word of explanation is needed.

First, let it be clearly and definitely stated, the purpose of this book is to maintain and improve the home. Criticism there is, deep and thorough; but not with the intention of robbing us of one essential element of home life—rather of saving us from conditions not only unessential, but gravely detrimental to home life. Every human being should have a home; the single person his or her home; and the family their home.

The home should offer to the individual rest, peace, quiet, comfort, health, and that degree of personal expression requisite; and these conditions should be maintained by the best methods of the time. The home should be to the child a place of happiness and true development; to the adult a place of happiness and that beautiful reinforcement of the spirit needed by the world's workers.

[3]

THE HOME

We are here to perform our best service to society, and to find our best individual growth and expression; a right home is essential to both these uses.

The place of childhood's glowing memories, of youth's ideals, of the calm satisfaction of mature life, of peaceful shelter for the aged; this is not attacked, this we shall not lose, but gain more universally. What is here asserted is that our real home life is clogged and injured by a number of conditions which are not necessary, which are directly inimical to the home; and that we shall do well to lay these aside.

As to the element of sanctity—that which is really sacred can bear examination, no darkened room is needed for real miracles; mystery and shadow belong to jugglers, not to the truth.

The home is a human institution. All human institutions are open to improvement. This specially dear and ancient one, however, we have successfully kept shut, and so it has not improved as have some others.

The home is too important a factor in human life to be thus left behind in the march of events; its influence is too wide, too deep, too general, for us to ignore.

Whatever else a human being has to meet and bear, he has always the home as a governing factor in the formation of character and the direction of life.

[4]

INTRODUCTORY

This power of home-influence we cannot fail to see, but we have bowed to it in blind idolatry as one of unmixed beneficence, instead of studying with jealous care that so large a force be wisely guided and restrained.

We have watched the rise and fall of many social institutions, we have seen them change, grow, decay, and die; we have seen them work mightily for evil—or as mightily for good; and have learned to judge and choose accordingly, to build up and to tear down for the best interests of the human race.

In very early times, when the child-mind of inexperienced man was timid, soft, and yet conservative as only the mind of children and savages can be, we regarded all institutions with devout reverence and fear.

Primitive man bowed down and fell upon his face before almost everything, whether forces of nature or of art. To worship, to enshrine, to follow blindly, was instinctive with the savage.

The civilised man has a larger outlook, a clearer, better-ordered brain. He bases reverence on knowledge, he loses fear in the light of understanding; freedom and self-government have developed him. It does not come so readily to him to fall upon his face—rather he lifts his face bravely to see and know and do. In place of the dark and cruel superstitions of old time, with the crushing weight of a strong cult of priests, we have a free and growing church, branching steadily wider as more minds differ, and coming nearer always to that final merging of religion in life which shall leave them indistinguishable. In place of the iron despotisms of old time we have a similar growth and change in governments, approaching always nearer to a fully self-governing condition. Our growth has been great, but it has been irregular and broken by strange checks and reversions; also accompanied, even in its heights, by parallel disorders difficult to account for.

In all this long period of progress the moving world has carried with it the unmoving home; the man free, the woman confined; the man specialising in a thousand industries, the woman still limited to her domestic functions. We have constantly believed that this was the true way to live, the natural way, the only way. Whatever else might change—and all things did—the home must not. So sure were we, and are we yet, of this, that we have utterly refused to admit that the home has changed, has grown, has improved, in spite of our unshaken convictions and unbending opposition.

The softest, freest, most pliable and changeful living substance is the brain—the hardest and most iron-bound

as well. Given a sufficiently deep conviction, and facts
are but as dreams before its huge reality.

Our convictions about the home go down to the utter-
most depths, and have changed less under the tooth of
time than any others, yet the facts involved have altered
most radically. The structure of the home has changed
from cave to tent, from tent to hut, from hut to house,
from house to block or towering pile of " flats "; the
functions of the home have changed from every incipient
industry known to past times, to our remaining few; the
inmates of the home have changed, from the polygamous
group and its crowd of slaves, to the one basic family relation of father, mother, and child; but our feelings have
remained the same.

The progress of society we have seen to be hindered
by many evils in the world about us and in our own
characters; we have sought to oppose them as best we
might, and even in some degree to study them for wiser
opposition.

Certain diseases we have traced to their cause, removed
the cause, and so avoided the disease; others we are just
beginning to trace, as in our present warfare with " the
white plague," tuberculosis.

Certain forms of vice we are beginning to examine
similarly, and certain defects of character; we are learn-

ing that society is part of the living world and comes under the action of natural law as much as any other form of life.

But in all this study of social factors affecting disease and vice and character, we have still held that the home—our most universal environment—was perfect and quite above suspicion.

We were right at bottom. The home *in its essential nature* is pure good, and in its due development is progressively good; but it must change with society's advance; and the kind of home that was wholly beneficial in one century may be largely evil in another. We must forcibly bear in mind, in any honest study of a long-accustomed environment, that our own comfort, or even happiness, in a given condition does not prove it to be good.

Comfort and happiness are very largely a matter of prolonged adjustment. We like what we are used to. When we get used to something else we like that too—and if the something else is really better, we profit by the change. To the tired farmer it is comfort to take off his coat, put up his yarn-stockinged feet on a chair, and have his wife serve him the supper she has cooked. The tired banker prefers a dressing gown or lounging jacket, slippers, a well-dressed, white-handed wife, and a neat

maid or stately butler to wait on the table. The
domestic Roman preferred a luxurious bath at the hands
of his slaves. All these types find comfort in certain
surroundings—yet the surroundings differ.

The New England farmer would not think a home
comfortable that was full of slaves—even a butler he
would find oppressive; the New York banker would not
enjoy seeing his wife do dirty work. Ideals change—
even home ideals; and whatever kind of home we have,
so that we grow up in it and know no other, we learn to
love. Even among homes as they now are, equally enjoyed by their inmates, there is a wide scale of difference. Why, then, is it impossible to imagine something
still further varying from what we now know;
yet to the children born therein as dear and deeply
loved?

Again let us remember that happiness, mere physical
comfort and the interchange of family affection, is not
all that life is for. We may have had " a happy childhood," as far as we can recall; we may have been idol-
ised and indulged by our parents, and have had no wish
ungratified; yet even so all this is no guarantee that the
beloved home has given us the best training, the best
growth. Nourmahal, the Light of the Harem, no doubt
enjoyed herself—but perhaps other surroundings might

have done more for her mind and soul. The questions raised here touch not only upon our comfort and happiness in such homes as are happy ones, but on the formative influence of these homes; asking if our present home ideals and home conditions are really doing all for humanity that we have a right to demand. There is a difference in homes not only in races, classes, and individuals, but in periods.

The sum of the criticism in the following study is this: the home has not developed in proportion to our other institutions, and by its rudimentary condition it arrests development in other lines. Further, that the two main errors in the right adjustment of the home to our present life are these: the maintenance of primitive industries in a modern industrial community, and the confinement of women to those industries and their limited area of expression. No word is said against the real home, the true family life; but it is claimed that much we consider essential to that home and family life is not only unnecessary, but positively injurious.

The home is a beautiful ideal, but have we no others? "My Country" touches a deeper chord than even "Home, Sweet Home." A homeless man is to be pitied, but "The Man without a Country" is one of the horrors of history. The love of mother and child is beautiful; but there is a higher law than that—the love of one another.

In our great religion we are taught to love and serve all mankind. Every word and act of Christ goes to show the law of universal service. Christian love goes out to all the world; it may begin, but does not stay, at home.

The trend of all democracy is toward a wider, keener civic consciousness; a purer public service. All the great problems of our times call for the broad view, the large concept, the general action. Such gain as we have made in human life is in this larger love; in some approach to peace, safety, and world-wide inter-service; yet this so patent common good is strangely contradicted and off-set by cross-currents of primitive selfishness. Our own personal lives, rich as they are to-day, broad with the consciousness of all acquainted races, deep with the consciousness of the uncovered past, strong with our universal knowledge and power; yet even so are not happy. We are confused—bewildered. Life is complicated, duties conflict, we fly and fall like tethered birds, and our new powers beat against old restrictions like ships in dock, fast moored, yet with all sail set and steam up.

It is here suggested that one cause for this irregular development of character, this contradictory social action, and this wearing unrest in life lies unsuspected in our homes; not in their undying essential factors, but in those phases of home life we should have long since peacefully outgrown. Let no one tremble in fear of losing precious things. That which is precious remains and will remain always. We do small honour to nature's laws when we imagine their fulfilment rests on this or that petty local custom of our own.

We may all have homes to love and grow in without the requirement that half of us shall never have anything else. We shall have homes of rest and peace for all, with no need for half of us to find them places of ceaseless work and care. Home and its beauty, home and its comfort, home and its refreshment to tired nerves, its inspiration to worn hearts, this is in no danger of loss or change; but the home which is so far from beautiful, so wearing to the nerves and dulling to the heart, the home life that means care and labour and disappointment, the quiet, unnoticed whirlpool that sucks down youth and beauty and enthusiasm, man's long labour and woman's longer love—this we may gladly change and safely lose. To the child who longs to grow up and be free; to the restless, rebelling boy; to the girl who marries all too hastily as a means of escape; to the man who puts his neck in the collar and pulls while life lasts to meet the unceasing demands of his little sanctuary; and to the woman—the thousands upon thousands of women, who work while life lasts to serve that sanctuary by night and day—to all these it may not be unwelcome to suggest that the home need be neither a prison, a workhouse, nor a consuming fire.

Home—with all that the sweet word means; home for each of us, in its best sense; yet shorn of its inordinate expenses, freed of its grinding labours, open to the blessed currents of progress that lead and lift us all— this we may have and keep for all time.

It is, therefore, with no iconoclastic frenzy of destruction, but as one bravely pruning a most precious tree, that this book is put forward; inquiring as to what is and what is not vital to the subject; and claiming broadly that with such and such clinging masses cut away, the real home life will be better established and more richly fruitful for good than we have ever known before.

II

THE EVOLUTION OF THE HOME

WE have been slow, slow and reluctant, to apply the laws of evolution to the familiar facts of human life. Whatever else might move, we surely were stationary; we were the superior onlookers—not part of the procession. Ideas which have possessed the racial mind from the oldest times are not to be dispossessed in a day; and this idea that man is something extra in the scheme of creation is one of our very oldest. We have always assumed that we were made by a special order, and that our manners and customs were peculiarly and distinctively our own, separated by an immeasurable gap from those of " the lower animals."

Now it appears, in large succeeding waves of proof, that there are no gaps in the long story of earth's continual creation; some pages may be lost to us, but they were once continuous. There is no break between us and the first stir of life upon our planet. Life is an unbroken line, a ceaseless stream that pours steadily on; or rather, it grows like an undying tree, some of whose branches wither and drop off, some reach their limit part way up, but the main trunk rises ever higher. We stand at the top and continue to grow, but we still carry with us many of the characteristics of the lower branches.

At what point in this long march of life was introduced that useful, blessed thing—the home? Is it something new, something distinctively human, like the church, the school, or the post office? No. It is traceable far back of humanity, back of the mammals, back of the vertebrates; we find it in most elaborate form even among insects.

What is a home? The idea of home is usually connected with that of family, as a place wherein young are born and reared, a common shelter for the reproductive group. The word may be also applied to the common shelter for any other permanent group, and to the place where any individual habitually stays. Continuous living in any place by individual or group makes that place a home; even old prisoners, at last released, have been known to come back to the familiar cell because it seemed like " home " to them. But " the home," in the sense in which we here discuss it, is the shelter of the family, of the group organised for purposes of reproduction. In this sense a beehive is as much a home as any human dwelling place—even more, perhaps. The snow hut of the Eskimo, the tent of hides that covers the American savage, the rock-bound fastness of the cave-dweller—these are homes as truly as the costliest modern mansion. The burrow of the prairie dog is a home, a fox's earth is a home, a bird's nest is a home, and the shelter of the little " seahorse " is a home. Wherever the mother feeds and guards her little ones,—more especially if the father helps her,—there is, for the time being, home.

This accounts at once for the bottomless depths of our attachment to the idea. For millions and millions of years it has been reborn in each generation and maintained by the same ceaseless pressure. The furry babies of the forest grow to consciousness in nests of leaves, in a warm stillness where they are safe and comfortable, where mother is—and mother is heaven and earth to the baby. Our lightly spoken phrase " What is home without a mother? " covers the deepest truth; there would never have been any home without her. It is from these antecedents that we may trace the formation of this deep-bedded concept, home.

The blended feelings covered by the word are a group of life's first necessities and most constant joys: shelter, quiet, safety, warmth, ease, comfort, peace, and love. Add to these food, and you have the sum of the animal's gratification. Home is indeed heaven to him. The world outside is, to the animal with a home, a field of excitement, exertion, and danger. He goes out to eat, in more or less danger of being eaten; but if he can secure his prey and drag it home he is then perfectly happy. Often he must feed where it falls, but then home is the place for the after-dinner nap.

With the graminivora there is no thought of home. The peaceful grass-eater drops foal or fawn, kid, calf, or lamb, where chance may find her in the open, and feeds at random under the sky. Vegetable food of a weak quality like grass has to be constantly followed up; there is no time to gather armfuls to take home, even if there were homes—or arms. But the beasts of prey have homes and love them, and the little timid things that live in instant danger—they, too, have homes to hide in at a moment's notice. These deep roots of animal satisfaction underlie the later growths of sentiment that so enshrine the home idea with us. The retreat, the shelter both from weather and enemies, this is a primal root.

It is interesting to note that there is a strong connection still between a disagreeable climate and the love of home. Where it is comfortable and pleasant out of doors, then you find the life of the street, the market place, the café, the plaza. Where it is damp and dark and chill, where rain and wind, snow and ice make it unpleasant without, there you find people gathering about the fireside, and boasting of it as a virtue—merely another instance of the law that makes virtue of necessity.

Man began with the beasts' need of home and the beasts' love of home. To this he rapidly applied new needs and new sentiments. The ingenious ferocity of man, and his unique habit of preying on his own kind, at once introduced a new necessity, that of fortification. Many animals live in terror of attack from other kinds of animals, and adapt their homes defensively as best they may, but few are exposed to danger of attack from their own kind. Ants, indeed, sometimes make war; bees are sometimes thieves; but man stands clear in his preeminence as a destroyer of his own race. From this habit of preying on each other came the need of fortified homes, and so the feeling of safety attached to the place grew and deepened.

The sense of comfort increased as we learned to multiply conveniences, and, with this increase in conveniences, came decreased power to do without them. The home where all sat on the floor had not so much advantage in comfort over " out-of-doors " as had the home where all sat on chairs, and became unable to sit on the ground with ease. So safety and comfort grew in the home concept. Shelter, too, became more complex as door and window and curtain guarded us better, and made us more susceptible to chill. Peace became more dear at home as war increased outside; quiet, as life waxed louder in the world; love, as we learned to hate each other more. The more dangerous and offensive life outside, the more we cling to the primal virtues of the home; and conversely, in our imagination of heaven, we do not picture the angels as bound up in their homes—if, indeed, they have any—but as gladly mingling in the larger love which includes them all. When we say " Heaven is my home," we mean the whole of it.

The care and shelter of the young is a far larger problem with us than with our hairy ancestors. Our longer period of immaturity gives us monogamous marriage and the permanent home. The animal may change his mate and home between litters; ours lap. This overlapping, long-continuing babyhood has given us more good than we yet recognise.

Thus we see that all the animal cared for in the home we have in greater degree, and care for more; while we have, further, many home ideals they knew not. One of the earliest steps in human development was ancestor-worship. With lower animals the parents do their duty cheerfully, steadily, devotedly, but there is no thought of return. The law of reproduction acts to improve the race by relentlessly sacrificing the individual, and that individual, the parent, never sets up a claim to any special veneration or gratitude.

But with us it is different. Our little ones lasting longer and requiring more care, we become more conscious of our relation to them. So the primitive parent very soon set up a claim upon the child, and as the child was absolutely helpless and in the power of the parent, it did not take long to force into the racial mind this great back-acting theory. The extreme height is found where it is made a religion, ancestor-worship, once very common, and still dominant in some of our oldest, *i. e.,* most primitive civilisations, as the Chinese. This ancestor-worship is what gave the element of sanctity to the home. As late as the Roman civilisation its power was so strong that the home was still a temple to a dwindling group of household gods—mere fossil grandpas—and we ourselves are not yet free from the influence of Roman civilisation. We still talk in poetic archaisms of " the altar of the home."

The extension of the family from a temporary reproductive group to a permanent social group is another human addition to the home idea. To have lived in one hole all his infancy makes that hole familiar and dear to the little fox. To have lived in one nest all his life makes that nest more familiar and more dear to the rook. But to have lived in one house for generations, to have " the home of my ancestors " loom upon one's growing consciousness—this is to enlarge enormously our sense of the dignity and value of the term.

This development of the home feeling of course hinges upon the theory of private property rights; and on another of our peculiar specialties, the exaltation of blood-relationships. Our whole social structure, together with social progress and social action, rests in reality on social relationship—that is, on the interchange of special services between individuals. But we, starting the custom at a time when we knew no better, and perpetuating it blindly, chose to assume that it was more important to be connected physically as are the animals, than psychically as human beings; so we extended the original family group of father, mother, and child into endless collateral lines and tried to attach our duties, our ambitions, our virtues and achievements to that group exclusively. The effect of this on any permanent home was necessarily to still further enlarge and deepen the sentiment attached to it.

There is another feature of human life, however, which

has contributed enormously to our home sentiment,—the position of women. Having its rise, no doubt, in the overlapping babyhood before mentioned, the habit grew of associating women more continuously with the home, but this tendency was as nothing compared to the impetus given by the custom of ownership in women. Women became, practically, property. They were sold, exchanged, given and bequeathed like horses, hides, or weapons. They belonged to the man, as did the house; it was one property group. With the steadily widening gulf between the sexes which followed upon this arbitrary imprisonment of the woman in the home, we have come to regard " the world " as exclusively man's province, and " the home " as exclusively woman's.

The man, who constitutes the progressive wing of the human race, went on outside as best he might, organising society, and always enshrining in his heart the woman and the home as one and indivisible. This gives the subtle charm of sex to a man's home ideals, and, equally, the scorn of sex to a man's home practices. Home to the man first means mother, as it does to all creatures, but later, and with renewed intensity, it means his own private harem—be it never so monogamous—the secret place where he keeps his most precious possession.

Thus the word " home," in the human mind, touches

the spring of a large complex group of ideas and sentiments, some older than humanity, some recent enough
for us to trace their birth, some as true and inalienable
as any other laws of life, some as false and unnecessary as
any others of mankind's mistakes. It does not follow
that all the earliest ones are right for us to-day, because
they were right for our remote predecessors, or that those
later introduced are therefore wrong.

What is called for is a clear knowledge of the course
of evolution of this earliest institution and an understanding of the reasons for its changes, that we may discriminate to-day between that which is vital and permanent in home life and that which is unessential and injurious. We may follow without difficulty the evolution
of each and all the essential constituents of home, mark
the introduction of non-essentials, show the evils resultant
from forced retention of earlier forms; in a word, we may
study the evolution of the home precisely as we study
that of any other form of life.

Take that primal requisite of safety and shelter which
seems to underlie all others, a place where the occupant
may be protected from the weather and its enemies. This
motive of home-making governs the nest-builder, the bur-
row-digger, the selecter of caves; it dominates the insect,
the animal, the savage, and the modern architect.

THE HOME

Dangers change, and the home must change to suit the danger. So after the caves were found insufficient, the lake-dwellers built above the water, safe when the bridge was in. The drawbridge as an element of safety lingered long, even when an artificial moat must needs be made for lack of lake. When the principal danger is cold, as in Arctic regions, the home is built thick and small; when it is heat, we build thick and large; when it is dampness, we choose high ground, elevate the home, lay drains; when it is wind, we seek a sheltered slope, or if there is no slope, plant trees as a wind-break to protect the home, or, in the worst cases, make a " cyclone cellar."

The gradual development of our careful plastering and glazing, our methods of heating, of carpeting and curtaining, comes along this line of security and shelter, modified always by humanity's great enemy, conservatism. In these mechanical details, as in deeper issues, free adaptation to changed conditions is hindered by our invariable effort to maintain older habits. Older habits are most dear to the aged, and as the aged have always most controlled the home, that institution is peculiarly slow to respond to the kindling influence of changed condition. The Chaldeans built of brick for years unnumbered, because clay was their only building material. When they spread into Assyria, where stone was plenty, they continued calmly putting up great palaces of sunbaked brick,—mere *adobe*,—and each new king left the cracking terraces of his predecessor's pride and built another equally ephemeral. The influence of our ancestors has dominated the home more than it has any other human institution, and the influence of our ancestors is necessarily retroactive.

In the gathering currents of our present-day social evolution, and especially in this country where progress is not feared, this heavy undertow is being somewhat overcome. Things move so rapidly now that one life' counts the changes, there is at last a sense of motion in human affairs, and so these healthful processes of change can have free way. The dangers to be met today by the home-builder are far different from those of ancient times, and, like most of our troubles, are largely of our own making. Earthquake and tidal wave still govern our choice of place and material somewhat, and climate of course always, but fire is the chief element of danger in our cities, and next to fire the greatest danger in the home is its own dirt.

The savage was dirty in his habits, from our point of view, but he lived in a clean world large enough to hold his little contribution of bones and ashes, and he did not defile his own tent with detritus of any sort. We, in our far larger homes, with our far more elaborate processes of living, and with our ancient system of confining women to the home entirely, have evolved a continuous accumulation of waste matter in the home. The effort temporarily to remove this waste is one of the main lines of domestic industry; the effort to produce it is the other.

Just as we may watch the course of evolution from a tiny transparent cell, absorbing some contiguous particle of food and eliminating its microscopic residuum of waste, up to the elaborate group of alimentary processes which make up so large a proportion of our complex physiology; so we may watch the evolution of these home processes from the simple gnawing of bones and tossing them in a heap of the cave-dweller, to the ten-course luncheon with its painted menu. In different nations the result varies, each nation assumes its methods to be right, and, so assuming, labours on to meet its supposed needs, to fulfil its local ambitions and duties as it apprehends them. And in no nation does it occur to the inhabitants to measure their habits and customs by the effect on life, health, happiness, and character.

The line of comfort may be followed in its growth like the line of safety. At first anything to keep the wind and rain off was comfortable—any snug hole to help retain the heat of the little animal. Then that old ABC of all later luxury, the bed, appeared—something soft between you and the rock—something dry between you and the ground. So on and on, as ease grew exquisite and skill increased, till we robbed the eider duck and stripped the goose to make down-heaps for our tender flesh to lie on, and so to the costly modern mattress. The ground, the stamped clay floor, the floor of brick, of stone, of wood; the rushes and the sand; the rug—a mere hide once and now the woven miracle of years of labour in the East, or gaudy carpet of the West—so runs that line of growth. Always the simple beginning, and its natural development under the laws of progress to more and more refinement and profusion. Always the essential changes that follow changed conditions, and always the downward pull of inviolate home-tradition, to hold back evolution when it could.

See it in furnishing: A stone or block of wood to sit on, a hide to lie on, a shelf to put the food on. See that block of wood change under your eyes and crawl up history on its forthcoming legs—a stool, a chair, a sofa, a settee, and now the endless ranks of sittable furniture wherewith we fill the home to keep ourselves from the floor withal. And these be-stuffed, be-springed, and up-holstered till it would seem as if all humanity were newly whipped. It is much more tiresome to stand than to walk.

THE HOME

If you are confined at home you cannot walk much—therefore you must sit—especially if your task be a stationary one. So, to the home-bound woman came much sitting, and much sitting called for ever softer seats, and to the wholly home-bound harem women even sitting is too strenuous; there you find cushions and more cushions and eternal lying down. A long way this from the strong bones, hard muscles, and free movement of the sturdy squaw, and yet a sure product of evolution with certain modifications of religious and social thought.

Our homes, thanks to other ideas and habits, are not thus ultra-cushioned; our women can still sit up, most of the time, preferring a stuffed chair. And among the more normal working classes, still largely and blessedly predominant, neither the sitting nor the stuffing is so evident. A woman who does the work in an ordinary home seldom sits down, and when she does any chair feels good.

In decoration this long and varied evolution is clearly and prominently visible, both in normal growth, in natural excess, and in utterly abnormal variations. So large a field of study is this that it will be given separate consideration in the chapter on Domestic Art.

What is here sought is simply to give a general impression of the continual flux and growth of the home as an institution, as one under the same laws as those which govern other institutions, and also of the check to that growth resultant from our human characteristic of remembering, recording, and venerating the past. The home, more than any other human phenomenon, is under that heavy check. The home is an incarnate past to us. It is our very oldest thing, and holds the heart more deeply than all others. The conscious thought of the world is always far behind the march of events, it is most so in those departments where we have made definite efforts to keep it at an earlier level, and nowhere, not even in religion, has there been a more distinct, persistent, and universal attempt to maintain the most remote possible status.

" The tendency to vary," that inadequate name for the great centrifugal force which keeps the universe swinging, is manifested most in the male. He is the natural variant, where the female is the natural conservative. By forcibly combining the woman with the home in his mind, and forcibly compelling her to stay there in body, then, conversely, by taking himself out and away as completely as possible, we have turned the expanding lines of social progress away from the home and left the ultra-feminised woman to ultra-conservatism therein. Where this condition is most extreme, as in the Orient, there is least progress; where it is least extreme, as with us, there is the most progress; but even with us, the least evolved of all our institutions is the home. Move it must, somewhat, as part of human life, but the movement has come from without, through the progressive man, and has been sadly retarded in its slow effect on the stationary woman.

This difference in rate of progress may be observed in the physical structure of the home, in its industrial processes, and in the group of concepts most closely associated with it. We have run over, cursorily enough, the physical evolution of the home-structure, yet wide as have been its changes they do not compare with the changes along similar lines in the ultra-domestic world. Moreover, such changes as there are have been introduced by the free man from his place in the more rapidly progressive world outside.

The distinctively home-made product changes far less. We see most progress in the physical characteristics of the home, its plan, building, materials, furnishings, and decoration, because all these are part of the world growth outside. We see less progress in such of the home industries as remain to us. It should be always held in mind that the phrase " domestic industry " does not apply to a special kind of work, but to a certain grade of work, a stage of development through which all kinds pass. All industries were once " domestic," that is, were

EVOLUTION OF THE HOME
performed at home and in the interests of the family.
All industries have since that remote period risen to
higher stages, except one or two which are still classed as
" domestic," and rightly so, since they are the only industries on earth which have never left their primal stage.
This a very large and important phase of the study of
the home, and will be given due space later.

Least of all do we see progress in the home ideas. The
home has changed much in physical structure, in spite of
itself. It has changed somewhat in its functions, also in
spite of itself. But it has changed very little—painfully
little—dangerously little, in its governing concepts.
Naturally ideas change with facts, but if ideas are held
to be sacred and immovable, the facts slide out from
under and go on growing because they must, while the
ideas lag further and further behind. We once held
that the earth was flat. This was our concept and governed our actions. In time, owing to a widening field
of action on the one hand, and a growth of the human
brain on the other, we ascertained the fact that the earth
was round. See the larger thought of Columbus driving
him westward, while the governing concepts of the sailors, proving too strong for him, dragged him back.
Then, gradually, with some difficulty, the idea followed
the fact, and has since penetrated to all minds in civil-

[31]

ised countries. But the flatness of the earth was not an essential religious concept, though it was clung to strongly by the inert religion of the time; nor was it a domestic concept, something still more inert. If it had been, it would have taken far longer to make the change.

What progress has been made in our domestic concepts? The oldest,—the pre-human,—shelter, safety, comfort, quiet, and mother love, are still with us, still crude and limited. Then follow gradually later sentiments of sanctity, privacy, and sex-seclusion; and still later, some elements of personal convenience and personal expression. How do these stand as compared with the facts? Our safety is really insured by social law and order, not by any system of home defence. Against the real dangers of modern life the home is no safeguard. It is as open to criminal attack as any public building, yes, more. A public building is more easily and effectively watched and guarded than our private homes. Sewer gas invades the home; microbes, destructive insects, all diseases invade it also; so far as civilised life is open to danger, the home is defenceless. So far as the home is protected it is through social progress—through public sanitation enforced by law and the public guardians of the peace. If we would but shake off the primitive limitations of these old concepts, cease to imagine the home to be a safe place, and apply our ideas of shelter, safety, comfort, and quiet to the City and State, we should then be able to ensure their fulfilment in our private homes far more fully.

The mother-love concept suffers even more from its limitations. As a matter of fact our children are far more fully guarded, provided for, and educated, by social efforts than by domestic; compare the children of a nation with a system of public education with children having only domestic education; or children safeguarded by public law and order with children having only domestic protection. The home-love and care of the Armenians for their children is no doubt as genuine and strong as ours, but the public care is not strong and well organised, hence the little Armenians are open to massacre as little Americans are not. Our children are largely benefited by the public, and would be much more so if the domestic concept did not act too strongly in limiting mother love to so narrow a field of action.

The later sentiments of sanctity and the others have moved a little, but not much. *Why* it is more sacred to make a coat at home than to buy it of a tailor, to kill a cow at home than to buy it of a butcher, to cook a pie at home than to buy it of a baker, or to teach a child at home than to have it taught by a teacher, is not made

clear to us, but the lingering weight of those ages of
ancestor-worship, of real sacrifice and libation at a real
altar, is still heavy in our minds. We still by race-habit
regard the home as sacred, and cheerfully profane our
halls of justice and marts of trade, as if social service
were not at least as high a thing as domestic service.
This sense of sanctity is a good thing, but it should grow,
it should evolve along natural lines till it includes all
human functions, not be forever confined to its cradle,
the home.

The concept of sex-seclusion is, with us, rapidly passing away. Our millions of wage-earning women are leading us, by the irresistible force of accomplished fact, to
recognise the feminine as part of the world around us,
not as a purely domestic element. The foot-binding
process in China is but an extreme expression of this old
domestic concept, the veiling process another. We are
steadily leaving them all behind, and an American man
feels no jar to his sexuo-domestic sentiments in meeting
a woman walking freely in the street or working in the
shops.

The latest of our home-ideas, personal convenience and
expression, are themselves resultant from larger development of personality, and lead out necessarily. The accumulating power of individuality developed in large

social processes by the male, is inherited by the female; she, still confined to the home, begins to fill and overfill it with the effort at individual expression, and must sooner or later come out to find the only normal field for highly specialised human power—the world.

Thus we may be encouraged in our study of domestic evolution. The forces and sentiments originating in the home have long since worked out to large social processes. We have gone far on our way toward making the world our home. What most impedes our further progress is the persistent retention of certain lines of industry within domestic limits, and the still more persistent retention of certain lines of home feelings and ideas. Even here, in the deepest, oldest, darkest, slowest place in all man's mind, the light of science, the stir of progress, is penetrating. The world does move—and so does the home.

III

DOMESTIC MYTHOLOGY

THERE is a school of myths connected with the home, more tenacious in their hold on the popular mind than even religious beliefs. Of all current superstitions none are deeper rooted, none so sensitive to the touch, so acutely painful in removal. We have lived to see nations outgrow some early beliefs, but others are still left us to study, in their long slow processes of decay. Belief in " the divine right of kings," for instance, is practically outgrown in America; and yet, given a king,—or even a king's brother,—and we show how much of the feeling remains in our minds, disclaim as we may the idea. Habits of thought persist through the centuries; and while a healthy brain may reject the doctrine it no longer believes, it will continue to feel the same sentiments formerly associated with that doctrine.

Wherever the pouring stream of social progress has had little influence,—in remote rural regions, hidden valleys, and neglected coasts,—we find still in active force some of the earliest myths. They may change their names as new religions take the place of old, Santa Claus and St. Valentine holding sway in place of forgotten deities of dim antiquity, but the festival or custom embodied is the same that was enjoyed by those most primitive ancestors. Of all hidden valleys none has so successfully avoided discovery as the Home. Church and State might change as they would—as they must; science changed, art changed, business changed, all human functions changed and grew save those of the home. Every man's home was his castle, and there he maintained as far as possible the facts and fancies of the place, unaltered from century to century.

The facts have been too many for him. The domestic hearth, with its undying flame, has given way to the gilded pipes of the steam heater and the flickering evanescence of the gas range. But the sentiment about the domestic hearth is still in play. The original necessity for the ceaseless presence of the woman to maintain that altar fire—and it was an altar fire in very truth at one period—has passed with the means of prompt ignition; the matchbox has freed the housewife from that incessant service, but the *feeling* that women should stay at home is with us yet.

The time when all men were enemies, when out-of-doors was one promiscuous battlefield, when home, well fortified, was the only place on earth where a man could rest in peace, is past, long past. But the *feeling* that home is more secure and protective than anywhere else is not outgrown.

So we have quite a list of traditional sentiments connected with home life well worth our study; not only for their interest as archæological relics, but because of their positive injury to the life of to-day, and in the hope that a fuller knowledge will lead to sturdy action. So far we have but received and transmitted this group of myths, handed down from the dim past; we continue to hand them down in the original package, never looking to see if they are so; if we, with our twentieth-century brains really believe them.

A resentful shiver runs through the reader at the suggestion of such an examination. "What! Scrutinise the home, that sacred institution, and even question it? Sacrilegious!" This very feeling proves the frail and threadbare condition of this group of ideas. Good healthy young ideas can meet daylight and be handled, but very old and feeble ones, that have not been touched for centuries, naturally dread inspection, and no wonder —they seldom survive it.

Let us begin with one especially dominant domestic myth, that fondly cherished popular idea—" the privacy of the home." In the home who has any privacy? Privacy means the decent seclusion of the individual, the right to do what one likes unwatched, uncriticised, unhindered. Neither father, mother, nor child has this right at home. The young man setting up in " chambers," the young woman in college room or studio, at last they realise what privacy is, at last they have the right to be alone. The home does provide some privacy for the family as a lump—but it remains a lump—there is no privacy for the individual. When homes and families began this was enough, people were simple, unspecialised, their tastes and wishes were similar; it is not enough to-day.

The progressive socialisation of humanity develops individuals; and this ever-increasing individuality suffers cruelly in the crude familiarity of home life. There sits the family, all ages, both sexes, as many characters as persons; and every budding expression, thought, feeling, or action has to run the gauntlet of the crowd. Suppose any member is sufficiently strong to insist on a place apart, on doing things alone and without giving information thereof to the others—is this easy in the home? Is this relished by the family?

The father, being the economic base of the whole structure, has most power in this direction; but in ninety-nine cases in a hundred he has taken his place and his work outside. In the one hundredth case, where some artist, author, or clergyman has to do his work at home—what is his opinion then of the privacy of that sacred place?

The artist flees to a studio apart, if possible; the author builds him a " den " in his garden, if he can afford it; the clergyman strives mightily to keep " the study " to himself, but even so the family, used to herding, finds it hard to respect anybody's privacy, and resents it.

The mother—poor invaded soul—finds even the bathroom door no bar to hammering little hands. From parlour to kitchen, from cellar to garret, she is at the mercy of children, servants, tradesmen, and callers. So chased and trodden is she that the very idea of privacy is lost to her mind; she never had any, she doesn't know what it is, and she cannot understand why her husband should wish to have any " reserves," any place or time, any thought or feeling, with which she may not make free.

The children, if possible, have less even than the mother. Under the close, hot focus of loving eyes, every act magnified out of all natural proportion by the close range, the child soul begins to grow. Noticed, studied, commented on, and incessantly interfered with; forced into miserable self-consciousness by this unremitting glare; our little ones grow up permanently injured in character by this lack of one of humanity's most precious rights—privacy.

The usual result, and perhaps the healthiest, is that bickering which is so distinctive a feature of family life. The effect varies. Sore from too much rubbing, there is a state of chronic irritability in the more sensitive; callous from too much rubbing there is a state of chronic indifference in the more hardy; and indignities are possible, yes, common, in family life which would shock and break the bonds of friendship or of love, and which would be simply inconceivable among polite acquaintances.

Another result, pleasanter to look at, but deeply injurious to the soul, is the affectionate dominance of the strongest member of the family; the more or less complete subservience of the others. Here is peace at least; but here lives are warped and stunted forever by the too constant pressure, close and heavy, surrounding them from infancy.

The home, as we know it, does not furnish privacy to the individual, rich or poor. With the poor there is such crowding as renders it impossible; and with the rich there is another factor so absolutely prohibitive of privacy that the phrase becomes a laughing-stock.

Private?—a place private where we admit to the most

intimate personal association an absolute stranger; or more than one? Strangers by birth, by class, by race, by education—as utterly alien as it is possible to conceive—these we introduce in our homes—in our very bedchambers; in knowledge of all the daily habits of our lives—and then we talk of privacy! Moreover, these persons can talk. As they are not encouraged to talk to us, they talk the more among themselves; talk fluently, freely, in reaction from the enforced repression of " their place," and, with perhaps a tinge of natural bitterness, revenging small slights by large comment. With servants living in our homes by day and night, confronted with our strange customs and new ideas, having our family affairs always before them, and having nothing else in their occupation to offset this interest, we find in this arrangement of life a condition as far removed from privacy as could be imagined.

Consider it further: The average servant is an ignorant young woman. Ignorant young women are proverbially curious, or old ones. This is not because of their being women, but because of their being ignorant. A well-cultivated mind has matter of its own to contemplate, and mental processes of absorbing interest. An uncultivated mind is comparatively empty and prone to unguarded gossip; its processes are crude and weak, the main faculty being an absorbing appetite for events —the raw material for the thoughts it cannot think. Hence the fondness of the servant class for " penny dreadfuls "—its preferred food is highly seasoned incident of a wholly personal nature. This is the kind of mind to which we offer the close and constant inspection of our family life. This is the kind of tongue which pours forth description and comment in a subdomiciliary stream. This is the always-open avenue of information for lover and enemy, spy and priest, as all history and literature exhibit; and to-day for the reporter— worse than all four.

In simple communities the women of the household, but little above the grade of servant in mind, freely gossip with their maids. In those more sophisticated we see less of this free current of exchange, but it is there none the less, between maid and maid, illimitable. Does not this prove that our ideas of privacy are somewhat crude—and that they are kept crude—must remain crude so long as the home is thus vulgarly invaded by low-class strangers? May we not hope for some development of home life by which we may outgrow forever these coarse old customs, and learn a true refinement which keeps inviolate the privacy of both soul and body in the home?

One other, yes, two other avenues of publicity are

open upon this supposed seclusion. We have seen that
the privacy of the mother is at the mercy of four sets of
invaders: children, servants, tradesmen, and callers.
The tradesmen, in a city flat, are kept at a pleasing
distance by the dumb-waiter and speaking tube; and,
among rich households everywhere, the telephone is a
defence. But, even at such long range, the stillness and
peace of the home, the chance to do quiet continued
work of any sort, are at the mercy of jarring electric bell
or piercing whistle. One of the joys of the country
vacation is the escape from just these things; the constant calls on time and attention, the interruption of
whatever one seeks to do, by these mercantile demands
against which the home offers no protection.

In less favoured situations, in the great majority of
comfortable homes, the invader gets far closer. "The
lady of the house" is demanded, and must come forth.
The front door opens, the back door yawns, the maid
pursues her with the calls of tradesmen, regular and irregular; from the daily butcher to the unescapable agent
with a visiting card. Of course we resist this as best
we may with a bulwark of trained servants. That is
one of the main uses of servants—to offer some protection to the inmates of this so private place, the home!

Then comes the fourth class—callers. A whole series

of revelations as to privacy comes here; a list so long and deep as to tempt a whole new chapter on that one theme. Here it can be but touched on, just a mention of the most salient points.

First there is the bulwark aforesaid, the servant, trained to protect a place called private from the entrance of a class of persons privileged to come in. To hold up the hands of the servant comes the lie; the common social lie, so palpable that it has no moral value to most of us—" Not at home! "

The home is private. Therefore, to be in private, you must claim to be out of it!

Back of this comes a whole series of intrenchments— the reception room, to delay the attack while the occupant hastily assumes defensive armour; the parlour or drawing room, wherein we may hold the enemy in play, cover the retreat of non-combatants, and keep some inner chambers still reserved; the armour above mentioned— costume and manner, not for the home and its inmates, but meant to keep the observer from forming an opinion as to the real home life; and then all the weapons crudely described in rural regions as " company manners," our whole system of defence and attack; by which we strive, and strive ever in vain, to maintain our filmy fiction of the privacy of the home.

THE HOME

The sanctity of the home is another dominant domestic myth. That we should revere the processes of nature as being the laws of God is good; a healthy attitude of mind. But why revere some more than others, and the lower more than the higher?

The home, as our oldest institution, is necessarily our lowest, it came first, before we were equal to any higher manifestation. The home processes are those which maintain the individual in health and comfort, or are intended to; and those which reproduce the individual. These are vital processes, healthy, natural, indispensable, but why sacred? To eat, to sleep, to breathe, to dress, to rest and amuse one's self—these are good and useful deeds; but are they more hallowed than others?

Then the shocked home-worshipper protests that it is not these physical and personal functions which he holds in reverence, but " the sacred duties of maternity," and " all those precious emotions which centre in the home."

Let us examine this view; but, first let us examine the sense of sanctity itself—see what part it holds in our psychology. In the first dawn of these emotions of reverence and sanctity, while man was yet a savage, the priest-craft of the day forced upon the growing racial mind a sense of darkness and mystery, a system of " tabu "—of " that which is forbidden." In China still, as term of high respect, the imperial seat of government is called " the Forbidden City." To the dim thick early mind, reverence was confounded with mystery and restriction.

To-day, in ever-growing light, with microscope and telescope and Röntgen ray, we are learning the true reverence that follows knowledge, and outgrowing that which rests on ignorance.

The savage reveres a thing because he cannot understand it—we revere because we can understand.

The ancient sacred must be covered up; to honour king or god you must shut your eyes, hide your face, fall prostrate.

The modern sacred must be shown and known of all, and honoured by understanding and observance.

Let not our sense of sanctity shrink so sensitively from the searcher; if the home is really sacred, it can bear the light. So now for these " sacred processes of reproduction." (Protest. " We did not say ' reproduction,' we said ' maternity ! ' ") And what is maternity but one of nature's processes of reproduction? Maternity and paternity and the sweet conscious duties and pleasures of human child-rearing are only more sacred than reproduction by fission, by parthenogenesis, by any other primitive device, because they are later in the course of evolution, so higher in the true measure of growth; and for that very reason education, the social function of child-rearing, is higher than maternity; later, more developed, more valuable, and so more sacred. Maternity is common to all animals—but we do not hold it sacred, in them. We have stultified motherhood most brutally in two of our main food products—milk and eggs—exploiting this function remorselessly to our own appetites.

In humanity, in some places and classes we do hold it sacred, however. Why? "Because it is the highest, sweetest, best thing we know!" will be eagerly answered. Is it—really? Is it better than Liberty, better than Justice, better than Art, Government, Science, Industry, Religion? How can that function which is common to savage, barbarian, peasant, to all kinds and classes, low and high, be nobler, sweeter, better, than those late-come, hard-won, slowly developed processes which make men greater, wiser, kinder, stronger from age to age?

The "sacred duties of maternity" reproduce the race, but they do nothing to improve it.

Is it not more sacred to teach right conduct for instance, as a true preacher does, than to feed one's own child as does the squaw? Grant that both are sacred—that all right processes are sacred—is not the relative sanctity up and out along the line of man's improvement?

Do we hold a wigwam more sacred than a beast's lair and less sacred than a modern home? If so, why? Do we hold an intelligent, capable mother more sacred than an ignorant, feeble one? Where are the limits and tendencies of these emotions?

The main basis of this home-sanctity idea is simply the historic record of our ancient religion of ancestor-worship. The home was once used as a church, as it yet is in China; and the odour of sanctity hangs round it still. The other basis is the equally old custom of sex-seclusion—the harem idea. This gives the feeling of mystery and " tabu," of " the forbidden "—a place shut and darkened—wholly private. A good, clean, healthy, modern home, with free people living and loving in it, is no more sacred than a schoolhouse. The schoolhouse represents a larger love, a higher function, a farther development for humanity. Let us revere, let us worship, but erect and open-eyed, the highest, not the lowest; the future, not the past!

Closely allied to our sense of home-sanctity and sprung from the same root, is our veneration for the old; either people or things; the " home of our ancestors " being if anything more sacred than our own, and the pot or plate or fiddle-back chair acquiring imputed sanctity by the simple flux of time. What time has to do with sanctity is not at first clear. Perhaps it is our natural respect for endurance. This thing has *lasted*, therefore it must be good; the longer it lasts the better it must be, let us revere it!

If this is a legitimate principle, let us hold pilgrimages to the primordial rocks, they have lasted longer than anything else, except sea water. Let us frankly worship the sun—or the still remoter dog-star. Let us revere the gar-fish above the shad—the hedgehog more than the cow—the tapir beyond the horse—they are all earlier types and yet endure!

Still more practically let us turn our veneration to the tools, vehicles, and implements which preceded ours —the arrow-head above the bullet, the bone-needle above the sewing machine, the hour-glass above the clock!

There is no genuine reason for this attitude. It is merely a race habit, handed down to us from very remote times and founded on the misconceptions of the ignorant early mind. The scientific attitude of mind is veneration of all the laws of nature, or works of God, as you choose to call them. If we must choose and distinguish, respecting this more than that, let us at least distinguish on right lines. The claim of any material object upon our respect is the degree of its use and beauty. A weak, clumsy, crooked tool acquires no sanctity from the handling of a dozen grandfathers; a good, strong, accurate one is as worthy of respect if made to-day. It is quite possible to the mind of man to worship idols, but it is not good for him.

A great English artist is said to have scorned visiting the United States of America as " a country where there were no castles." We might have showed him the work of the mound-builders, or the bones of the Triceratops, they are older yet. It will be a great thing for the human soul when it finally stops worshipping backwards. We are pushed forward by the social forces, reluctant and stumbling, our faces over our shoulder , clutching at every relic of the past as we are forced along; still adoring whatever is behind us. We insist upon worshipping " the God of our fathers." Why not the God of our children? Does eternity only stretch one way?

Another devoutly believed domestic myth is that of the " economy " of the home.

The man is to earn, and the woman to save, to expend judiciously, to administer the products of labour to the best advantage. We honestly suppose that our method of providing for human wants by our system of domestic economy is the cheapest possible; that it would cost more to live in any other way. The economic dependence of women upon men, with all its deadly consequences, is defended because of our conviction that her labour in the home is as productive as his out of it; that the marriage is a partnership in which, if she does not contribute in cash, she does in labour, care, and saving.

It is with a real sense of pain that one remorselessly punctures this beautiful bubble. When plain financial facts appear, when economic laws are explained, then it is shown that our " domestic economy " is the most wasteful department of life. The subject is taken up in detail in the chapter on home industries; here the mere statement is made, that the domestic system of feeding, clothing, and cleaning humanity costs more time, more strength, and more money than it could cost in any other way except absolute individual isolation. The most effort and the least result are found where each individual does all things for himself. The least effort and the most result are found in the largest specialisation and exchange.

The little industrial group of the home—from two to five or ten—is very near the bottom of the line of economic progress. It costs men more money, women more work, both more time and strength than need be by more than half. A method of living that wastes half the time and strength of the world is not economical.

Somewhat along this line of popular belief comes that pretty fiction about " the traces of a woman's hand." It is a minor myth, but very dear to us. We imagine that a woman—any woman—just because she is a woman, has an artistic touch, an æsthetic sense, by means of which she can cure ugliness as kings were supposed to cure scrofula, by the laying on of hands. We find this feelingly alluded to in fiction where some lonely miner, coming to his uncared-for cabin, discovers a flower pot, a birdcage and a tidy, and delightedly proclaims—" A woman has been here." He thinks it is beautiful because it is feminine—a sexuo-æsthetic confusion common to all animals.

The beauty-sense, as appealed to by sex-distinctions, is a strange field of study. The varied forms of crests, combs, wattles, callosities of blue and crimson, and the like, with which one sex attracts the other, are interesting to follow; but they do not appeal to the cultivated sense of beauty. Beauty—beauty of sky and sea, of flower and shell, of all true works of art—has nothing to do with sex.

When you turn admiring eyes on the work of those who *have* beautified the world for us; on the immortal

[53]

marbles and mosaics, vessels of gold and glass, on building and carving and modelling and painting; the enduring beauty of the rugs and shawls of India, the rich embroideries of Japan, you do not find in the great record of world-beauty such conspicuous traces of a woman's hand.

Then study real beauty in the home—any home—all homes. There are women in our farm-houses—women who painfully strive to produce beauty in many forms; crocheted, knitted, crazy-quilted, sewed together, stuck together, made of wax; made—of all awful things—of the hair of the dead! Here are traces of a woman's hand beyond dispute, but is it beauty? Through the hands of women, with their delighted approval, pours the stream of fashion without check. Fashion in furniture, fashion in china and glass, fashion in decoration, fashion in clothing. What miracle does " a woman's hand " work on this varying flood of change?

The woman is as pleased with black horsehair as with magenta reps; she is equally contented with " antimacassars " as with sofa-cushions, if these things are fashionable. Her " old Canton " is relegated to the garret when " French China " of unbroken white comes in; and then brought down again in triumph when the modern goes out and the antique comes in again.

DOMESTIC MYTHOLOGY

She puts upon her body without criticism or objection every excess, distortion, discord, and contradiction that can be sewed together. The æsthetic sense of woman has never interfered with her acceptance of ugliness, if ugliness were the fashion. The very hair of her head goes up and down, in and out, backwards and forwards under the sway of fashion, with no hint of harmony with the face it frames or the head it was meant to honour. In her house or on her person "the traces of a woman's hand" may speak loud of sex, and so please her opposite; but there is no assurance of beauty in the result. This sweet tradition is but another of our domestic myths.

Among them all, most prominent of all, is one so general and so devoutly accepted as to call for most thorough exposure. This is our beloved dogma of "the maternal instinct." The mother, by virtue of being a mother, is supposed to know just what is right for her children. We honestly believe, men and women both, that in motherhood inheres the power rightly to care for childhood.

This is a nature-myth, far older than humanity. We base the theory on observation of the lower animals. We watch the birds and beasts and insects, and see that the mother does all for the young; and as she has no instruction and no assistance, yet achieves her ends, we attribute her success to the maternal instinct.

What is an instinct? It is an inherited habit. It is an automatic action of the nervous system, developed in surviving species of many generations of repetition; and performing most intricate feats.

There is an insect which prepares for its young to eat a carefully paralysed caterpillar. This ingenious mother lays her eggs in a neatly arranged hole, then stings a caterpillar, so accurately as to deprive him of motion but not of life, and seals up the hole over eggs and fresh meat in full swing of the maternal instinct. A cruelly inquiring observer took out the helpless caterpillar as soon as he was put in; but the instinct-guided mother sealed up the hole just as happily. She had done the trick, as her instinct prompted, and there was no allowance for scientific observers in that prompting. She had no intelligence, only instinct. You may observe mother instinct at its height in a fond hen sitting on china eggs—instinct, but no brains.

We, being animals, do retain some rudiments of the animal instincts; but only rudiments. The whole course of civilisation has tended to develop in us a conscious intelligence, the value of which to the human race is far greater than instinct. Instinct can only be efficient in directing actions which are unvaryingly repeated by each individual for each occasion. It is that repetition which creates the instinct. When the environment of an animal changes he has to use something more than instinct, or he becomes ex-tinct!

The human environment is in continual flux, and changes more and more quickly as social evolution progresses. No personal conditions are so general and unvarying with us as to have time to develop an instinct; the only true ones for our race are the social instincts—and maternity is not a social process.

Education is a social process, the very highest. To collect the essentials of human progress and supply them to the young, so that each generation may improve more rapidly, that is education. The animals have no parallel to this. The education of the animal young by the animal mother tends only to maintain life, not to improve it. The education of a child, and by education is meant every influence which reaches it, from birth to maturity, is a far more subtle and elaborate process.

The health and growth of the body, the right processes of mental development, the ethical influences which shape character—these are large and serious cares, for which our surviving driblets of instinct make no provision. If there were an instinct inherent in human mothers sufficient to care rightly for their children, then all human mothers would care rightly for their children.

Do they?

What percentage of our human young live to grow up? About fifty per cent. What percentage are healthy? We do not even expect them to be healthy. So used are we to " infantile diseases " that our idea of a mother's duty is to nurse sick children, not to raise well ones! What percentage of our children grow up properly proportioned, athletic and vigorous? Ask the army surgeon who turns down the majority of applicants for military service. What percentage of our children grow up with strong, harmonious characters, wise and good? Ask the great army of teachers and preachers who are trying for ever and ever to somewhat improve the adult humanity which is turned out upon the world from the care of its innumerable mothers and their instincts.

Our eyes grow moist with emotion as we speak of our mothers—our own mothers—and what they have done for us. Our voices thrill and tremble with pathos and veneration as we speak of " the mothers of great men—" mother of Abraham Lincoln! Mother of George

DOMESTIC MYTHOLOGY

Washington! and so on. Had Wilkes Booth no mother? Was Benedict Arnold an orphan?

Who, in the name of all common sense, raises our huge and growing crop of idiots, imbeciles, cripples, defectives, and degenerates, the vicious and the criminal; as well as all the vast mass of slow-minded, prejudiced, ordinary people who clog the wheels of progress? Are the mothers to be credited with all that is good and the fathers with all that is bad?

That we are what we are is due to these two factors, mothers and fathers.

Our physical environment we share with all animals. Our social environment is what modifies heredity and develops human character. The kind of country we live in, the system of government, of religion, of education, of business, of ordinary social customs and convention, this is what develops mankind, this is given by our fathers.

What does maternal instinct contribute to this sum of influences? Has maternal instinct even evolved any method of feeding, dressing, teaching, disciplining, educating children which commands attention, not to say respect? It has not.

The mothers of each nation, governed only by this rudimentary instinct, repeat from generation to generation the mistakes of their more ignorant ancestors; like a dog turning around three times before he lies down on the carpet, because his thousand-remove progenitors turned round in the grass!

That the care and education of children have developed at all is due to the intelligent efforts of doctors, nurses, teachers, and such few parents as chose to exercise their human brains instead of their brute instincts.

That the care and education of children are still at the disgraceful level generally existent is due to our leaving these noble functions to the unquestioned dominance of a force which, even among animals, is not infallible, and which, in our stage of socialisation, is practically worthless.

Of all the myths which befog the popular mind, of all false worship which prevents us from recognising the truth, this matriolatry is one most dangerous. Blindly we bow to the word " mother "—worshipping the recreative processes of nature as did forgotten nations of old time in their great phallic religions.

The processes of nature are to be studied, not worshipped; the laws of nature find best reverence in our intelligent understanding and observance, not in obsequious adoration. When the human mother shows that she understands her splendid function by developing a free, strong, healthy body; by selecting a vigorous and noble mate; by studying the needs of childhood, and meeting them with proficient services, her own or that of others better fitted; by presenting to the world a race of children who do not die in infancy, who are not preyed upon by " preventable diseases," who grow up straight, strong, intelligent, free-minded, and right-intentioned; then we shall have some reason to honour motherhood, and it will be brain-work and soul-work that we honour. Intelligence, study, experience, science, love that has more than a physical basis—human motherhood—not the uncertain rudiments of a brute instinct!

IV

PRESENT CONDITIONS

THE difference between our current idea of the home to-day, and its real conditions, is easily seen. That is, it is easily seen if we are able temporarily to resist the pressure of inherited traditions, and use our individual brain power for a little while. We must remember, in attempting to look fairly, to see clearly, that a concept is a much stronger stimulus to the brain than a fact.

A fact, reaching the brain through any sensory nerve, is but an impression; and if a previous impression to the contrary exists, especially if that contrary impression has existed, untouched, for many generations, the fact has but a poor chance of acceptance. " What! " cries the astonished beholder of some new phenomenon. " Can I believe my eyes! " and he does not believe his eyes, preferring to believe the stock in trade of his previous ideas. It takes proof, much proof, glaring, positive, persistent, to convince us that what we have long thought to be so is not so. " A preconceived idea " is what we call this immoveable lump in the brain, and if the preconceived idea is deeply imbedded, knit, and rooted as an "underlying conviction," and has so existed for a very long time, then a bombardment of most undeniable facts bounds off it without effect.

Our ideas of the home are, as we have seen, among the very deepest in the brain; and to reach down into those old foundation feelings, to disentangle the false from the true, to show that the true home does not involve this group of outgrown rudiments is difficult indeed. Yet, if we will but use that wonderful power of thought which even the most prejudiced can exercise for a while, it is easy to see what are the real conditions of the average home to-day. By "average" is not meant an average of numbers. The world still has its millions of savage inhabitants who do not represent to-day, but anthropologic yesterdays, long past.

Even in our own nation, our ill-distributed social advance leaves us a vast majority of population who do not represent to-day, but a historic yesterday. The home that is really of to-day is the home of the people of to-day, those people who are abreast of the thought, the work, the movement of our times. The real conditions of the present-day home are to be studied here; not in the tepee of the Sioux, the clay-built walls of the Pueblo, the cabin of the "Georgia cracker," or moun-

taineer of Tennessee; or even in the thousand farm-
houses which still repeat so nearly the status of an earlier
time.

The growth and change of the home may be traced
through all these forms, in every stage of mechanical,
industrial, economic, artistic, and psychic development;
but the stage we need to study is that we are now in,
those homes which are pushed farthest in the forefront
of the stream of progress. An average home of to-day, in
this sense, is one of good social position, wherein the husband has sufficient means and the wife sufficient education to keep step with the march of events; one which
we should proudly point out to a foreign visitor as "a
typical American home."

Now, how does this home really stand under dispassionate observation?

The ideal which instantly obtrudes itself is this: A
beautiful, comfortable house meeting all physical needs;
a happy family, profoundly enjoying each other's society; a father, devotedly spending his life in obtaining
the wherewithal to maintain this little heaven; a
mother, completely wrapped up in her children and devotedly spending her life in their service, working miracles of advantage to them in so doing; children, happy
in the home and growing up beautifully under its benign

influence—everybody healthy, happy, and satisfied with the whole thing.

This ideal is what we are asked to lay aside temporarily; and in its place to bring our minds to bear on the palpable facts in the case. Readers of a specially accurate turn of mind may perhaps be interested enough to jot down on paper their own definite observations of, say, a dozen homes they know best.

One thing may be said here in defence of our general ignorance on this subject: the actual conditions of home life are studiously concealed from casual observation. Our knowledge of each other's homes is obtained principally by " calling " and the more elaborate forms of social entertainments.

The caller only reaches the specially prepared parlour or reception room; the more intimate friends sometimes the bedroom or even nursery, if they are at the time what we call " presentable "; and it is part of our convention, our age-long habit of mind, to accept this partial and prepared view as a picture of the home life. It is not.

To know any home really, you must live in it, " winter and summer " it, know its cellar as well as parlour, its daily habits as well as its company manners. So we have to push into the background not only the large, generally beautiful home ideal, smiling conventionally like a big bronze Buddha; but also that little pocket ideal which we are obliged to use constantly to keep up the proper mental attitude.

We are not used to looking squarely, open-eyed and critical, at any home, so "sacred" is the place to us. Now, having laid aside both the general ideal and the pocket ideal, what do we see?

As to physical health and comfort and beauty: Ask your Health Board, your sanitary engineer, how the laws of health are observed in the average home—even of the fairly well-to-do, even of the fairly educated. Learn what we may of art and science, the art of living, the science of living is not yet known to us. We build for ourselves elaborate structures in which to live, following architectural traditions, social traditions, domestic traditions, quite regardless of the laws of life for the creature concerned.

This home is the home of a live animal, a large animal, bigger than a sheep—about as big as a fallow deer. The comfort and health of this animal we seek to insure by first wrapping it in many thicknesses of cloth and then shutting it up in a big box, carefully lined with cloth and paper and occasionally "aired" by opening windows. We feed the animal in the box, bringing into it large and varied supplies of food, and cooking them there. Growing dissatisfied with the mess resultant upon this process, disliking the sight and sound and smell of our own preferred food-processes, yet holding it essential that they shall all be carried on in the same box with the animal to be fed; we proceed to enlarge the box into many varied chambers, to shut off by closed doors these offensive details (which we would not do without for the world), and to introduce into the box still other animals of different grades to perform the offensive processes.

You thus find in a first-class modern home peculiar warring conditions, in the adjustment of which health and comfort are by no means assured. The more advanced the home and its inhabitants, the more we find complexity and difficulty, with elements of discomfort and potential disease, involved in the integral—supposedly integral—processes of the place. The more lining and stuffing there are, the more waste matter fills the air and settles continually as dust; the more elaborate the home, the more labour is required to keep it fit for a healthy animal to live in; the more labour required, the greater the wear and tear on both the heads of the family.

The conditions of health in a representative modern

home are by no means what we are capable of compassing.

We consider " antiseptic cleanliness " as belonging only to hospitals, and are content to spend our daily, and nightly, lives in conditions of septic dirt.

An adult human being consumes six hundred cubic feet of air in an hour. How many homes provide such an amount, fresh, either by day or night?

Diseases of men may be attributed to exposure, to wrong conditions in shop and office, to chances of the crowd, or to special drug habits. Diseases of women and children must be studied at home, where they take rise. The present conditions of the home as to health and comfort are not satisfactory.

As to beauty : we have not much general knowledge of beauty, either in instinct or training ; yet, even with such as we have, how ill satisfied it is in the average home. The outside of the house is not beautiful ; the inside is not beautiful ; the decorations and furnishings are not beautiful. The home, by itself, in its age-long traditionalism, does not allow of growth in these lines ; nor do its physical limitations permit of it. But as education progresses and money accumulates we hire " art-decorators " and try to creep along the line of advance.

A true natural legitimate home beauty is rare indeed.

PRESENT CONDITIONS

We may be perfectly comfortable among our things, and even admire them; people of any race or age do that; but that sense of "a beautiful home" is but part of the complex ideal, not a fact recognised by those who love and study beauty and art. We do not find our common "interiors" dear to the soul of the painter. So we may observe that in general the home does not meet the demands of the physical nature, for simple animal health and comfort; nor of the psychical for true beauty.

Now for our happy family. Let it be carefully borne in mind that no question is raised as to the happiness of husband and wife; or of parent and child in their essential relation; but of their happiness as affected by the home.

The effect of the home, as it now is, upon marriage is a vitally interesting study. Two people, happily mated, sympathetic physically and mentally, having many common interests and aspirations, proceed after marrying to enter upon the business of "keeping house," or "home-making." This business is not marriage, it is not parentage, it is not child-culture. It is the running of the commissary and dormitory departments of life, with elaborate lavatory processes.

The man is now called upon to pay, and pay heavily,

for the maintenance of this group of activities; the
woman to work, either personally, by deputy, or both,
in its performance.

Then follows one of the most conspicuous of conditions in our present home: the friction and waste of its
supposedly integral processes. The man does spend his
life in obtaining the wherewithal to maintain—not a
"little heaven," but a bunch of ill-assorted trades,
wherein everything costs more than it ought to cost, and
nothing is done as it should be done—on a business
basis.

How many men simply hand out a proper sum of
money for "living expenses," and then live, serene and
steady, on that outlay?

Home expenses are large, uncertain, inexplicable. In
some families an exceptional "manager," provided with
with a suitable "allowance," does keep the thing in
comparatively smooth running order, at considerable
cost to herself; but in most families the simple daily
processes of "housekeeping" are a constant source of
annoyance, friction, waste, and loss. Housekeeping, as
a business, is not instructively successful. As the structure of the home is not what we so readily took for
granted in our easily fitting ideals, so the functions of
the home are not, either. We are really struggling and

fussing along, trying to live smoothly, healthfully, peacefully; studying all manner of " new thought " to keep us " poised," pining for a " simpler life "; and yet all spending our strength and patience on the endless effort to " keep house," to " make a home "—to live comfortably in a way which is not comfortable; and when this continuous effort produces utter exhaustion, we have *to go away from home* for a rest! Think of that, seriously.

The father is so mercilessly overwhelmed in furnishing the amount of money needed to maintain a home that he scarce knows what a home is. Time, time to sit happily down with his family, or to go happily out with his family, this is denied to the patient toiler on whose shoulders this ancient structure rests. The mother is so overwhelmed in her performance or supervision of all the inner workings of the place that she, too, has scant time for the real joys of family life.

The home is one thing, the family another; and when the home takes all one's time, the family gets little. So we find both husband and wife overtaxed and worried in keeping up the institution according to tradition; both father and mother too much occupied in home-making to do much toward child-training, man-making!

What is the real condition of the home as regards

children—its primal reason for being? How does the present home meet their needs? How does the home-bound woman fill the claims of motherhood? As a matter of fact, *are* our children happy and prosperous, healthy and good, at home? Again the ideal rises; picture after picture, tender, warm, glowing; again we must push it aside and look at the case as it is. In our homes to-day the child grows up—when he does not die—not at all in that state of riotous happiness we are so eager to assume as the condition of childhood. The mother loves the child, always and always; she does what she can, what she knows how; but the principal work of her day is the care of the house, not of the child; the construction of clothes—not of character.

Follow the hours in the day of the housewife: count the minutes spent in the care and service of the child, as compared with those given to the planning of meals, the purchase of supplies, the labour either of personally cleaning things or of seeing that other persons do it; the " duties " to society, of the woman exempt from the actual house-labour.

" But," we protest, " all this is for the child—the meals, the well-kept house, the clothes—the whole thing! "

Yes? And in what way do the meals we so elaborately order and prepare, the daintily furnished home, the much-trimmed clothing, contribute to the body-growth, mind-growth, and soul-growth of the child? The conditions of home life are not those best suited to the right growth of children. Infant discipline is one long struggle to coerce the growing creature into some sort of submission to the repressions, the exactions, the arbitrary conventions of the home.

In broad analysis, we find in the representative homes of to-day a condition of unrest. The man is best able to support it because he is least in it; he is part and parcel of the organised industries of the world, he has his own special business to run on its own lines; and he, with his larger life-basis, can better bear the pressure of house-worries. The wife is cautioned by domestic moralists not to annoy her husband with her little difficulties; but in the major part of them, the economic difficulties, she must consult him, because he pays the bills.

When a satisfactory Chinaman is running a household; when the money is paid, the care deputed, the whole thing done as by clock-work, this phase of home unrest is removed; but the families so provided for are few. In most cases the business of running a home is a source of constant friction and nervous as well as financial waste.

THE HOME

Quite beyond this business side come the conditions of home life, the real conditions, as affecting the lives of the inmates. With great wealth, and a highly cultivated taste, we find the members of the family lodged in as much privacy and freedom as possible in a home, and agreeing to disagree where they are not in accord. With great love and highly cultivated courtesy and wisdom, we find the members of the family getting on happily together, even in a physically restricted home. But in the average home, occupied by average people, we find the members of the family jarring upon one another in varying degree.

That harmony, peace, and love which we attribute to home life is not as common as our fond belief would maintain. The husband, as we have seen, finds his chief base outside, and bears up with greater or less success against the demands and anxieties of the home. The wife, more closely bound, breaks down in health with increasing frequency. The effect of home life on women seems to be more injurious in proportion to their social development. Our so-called "society" is one outlet, though not a healthful one, through which the woman seeks to find recreation, change, and stimulus to enable her to bear up against a too continuous home life.

PRESENT CONDITIONS

The young man at home is almost a negligible factor —he does not stay in it any more than he can help. The young woman at home finds her growing individuality an increasing disadvantage, and many times makes a too hasty marriage because she is not happy at home—in order to have " a home of her own," where she still piously believes all will be well.

The child at home has no knowledge of any other and better environment wherewith to compare this. He accepts his home as the unavoidable base of all things— he cannot think of life with a different home. But the eagerness with which he hails any proposition that takes him out of it, his passionate hunger for change, for novelty; the fever which most boys have for " running away "; the eager, intense interest in stories of anything and everything as far removed from home life as possible; the dreary *ennui* of the child who is punished by being kept at home—or who has to stay there continuously for any reason—standing at the window which can give sight of the world outside and longing for something to happen—all this goes to indicate that home life does not satisfy the child. There was a time when it did, when it satisfied every member of the family; but that was under far more primitive conditions.

The home has not developed in the same ratio as its

occupants. The people of to-day are not content in the homes of a thousand years before yesterday. Our present home conditions are being changed—very gradually, owing to the stiffness of the material, but are slowly changing before our eyes. As a matter of fact, we are ready—more than ready—for the homes of the future; as a matter of feeling, we are clinging with all our might to the homes of the past; and, in their present conditions, our homes are not by any means those centres of rest, peace, and satisfaction we are so religiously taught to think them.

Suppose for an instant that they were. Suppose the trouble, the weariness, the danger and evils of outside life were all laid aside the moment we entered the home. There all was well. No financial trouble. No industrial trouble. No physical trouble. No mental trouble. No moral trouble. Just a place where everything ran on wheels; and where the world-worn soul could count on peace and refreshment.

Vain supposition! Whatever the financial troubles of the world, the place where they are felt most is in the home. Here is where the money is spent, and most wastefully misspent as we shall see later. Here is where there is never enough, where the demand continually exceeds the supply.

PRESENT CONDITIONS

As to industrial trouble, the labour question is a large one everywhere. The introduction of machinery has brought its train of needless disadvantages as well as its essential advantages. There are dishonesty and inefficiency to meet and cope with. But compare the conversation of a hundred business men with that of a hundred housekeeping women, and learn respect for the magnitude of the industrial troubles of the home.

For physical troubles, as we have before indicated, the home is no relief. We struggle to enforce laws improving the physical conditions of the coal mine and the factory, but these laws find their utmost difficulty of application in the " sweatshops," the place where work is done at home. There is no law to improve the sanitary condition of the kitchen, to compel the admission of oxygen to the bedroom. In the home every law of health may be disregarded with impunity. We strive by building regulations and Boards of Health to make some improvement, but the conditions of home life, as now existing, are no guarantee of safety from physical troubles.

As to the mental and moral—the whole field of psychical error and difficulty—the home is the place where we suffer most. The struggles and falls of the soul, our most intimate sins, the keenest pain we know—

the home is the arena for these in large measure. Tender virtues grow there, too—deep and abiding love, generous devotion, patient endurance—faithfulness and care; but for one home that shows us these is another where dominant injustice, selfishness, unthinking cruelty, impatience, grossest rudeness, a callous disregard for the oft-trodden feelings of others is found instead. No wide acquaintance with present homes can fail to note these things in every shade of growth. Home is a place where people live, people good and bad, great and small, wise and unwise. The home does not make the bad good, the small great, or the foolish wise. Many a man who *has* to be decent in his social life is domineering and selfish at home. Many a woman who has to be considerate and polite in her social life, such as it is, is exacting and greedy at home, and cruel as only the weak and ignorant can be. Now if the home was what produced the virtues we commonly attribute to it, then all homes, of all times and peoples, would have the same effect.

The American man holds pre-eminence as sacrificed to the home; the American woman as being most petted and indulged therein. In England we find the man more the centre of indulgence, in Germany still more so—and the women subsidiary to his use and pleasure.

How can " the home " be credited with such opposite

results? If, as is commonly assumed, the home has any unfailing general effect, we must be able to point out that effect in the homes of Russia, China, France, and Egypt. If we find the homes of the nations differ we must look for the cause in the national institutions—not the domestic.

That our well-loved homes are as good as they are is due to our race progress; to our religion, our education, our general social advance. When a peasant family from Hungary comes to America, they establish a Hungarian home. As they become Americanised the home changes and improves. The credit is not due to the home, but to the country. Meanwhile the home does have certain definite effects upon our life; due to its own nature, and acting upon us in every time and place.

These we shall analyse and follow in studying the effects of the home upon society in a later chapter. In this observation of present conditions we should note merely how our average home life now stands. And we may plainly see these things: a general condition of unrest and more or less dissatisfaction. A tendency to ever-growing expense, which threatens the very existence of the home and is forcing many into boarding houses. An increasing difficulty in the industrial processes—a difficulty so great that the lives of our women are embittered

[79]

and shortened by it, and the periods of anxiety and ill-adjustment are longer than those of satisfactory service. An improvement in sanitary conditions so far as public measures can reach the home, but a wide field of disease owing to wrong habits of clothing, eating, and breathing. A rudimentary custom of child-culture only beginning to show signs of progress; and a degree of unhappiness to which the divorce and criminal courts, as well as insane asylums and graveyards, bear crushing testimony.

With conditions of home life as far from our cherished ideal as these, is it not time for us bravely to face the problem, and study home life with a view to its improvement? Not " to abolish the home," as is wildly feared by those who dare not discuss it. A pretty testimony this to their real honour and belief! Is the home so light a thing as to be blown away by a breath of criticism? Are we so loosely attached to our homes as to give them up when some defects are pointed out? Is it not a confession of the discord and pain we so stoutly deny, that we are not willing to pour light into this dark place and see what ails it?

There is no cause for fear. So long as life lasts we shall have homes; but we need not always have the same kind.

PRESENT CONDITIONS

Our present home is injured by the rigidly enforced maintenance of long-outgrown conditions. We may free ourselves, if we will, from every one of those injurious, old conditions, and still retain all that is good and beautiful and right in the home.

V

THE HOME AS A WORKSHOP

I. *The Housewife*

ALL industry began at home.

All industry was begun by women.

Back of history, at the bottom of civilisation, during that long period of slowly changing savagery which antedates our really human life, whatever work was done on earth was done by the woman in the home. From that time to this we have travelled far, spread wide, grown broad and high; and our line of progress is the line of industrial evolution.

Where the patient and laborious squaw once carried on her back the slaughtered game for her own family, now wind and steam and lightning distribute our provisions around the world. Where she once erected a rude shelter of boughs or hides for her own family, now mason and carpenter, steel and iron worker, joiner, lather, plasterer, glazier, plumber, locksmith, painter, and decorator combine to house the world. Where she chewed and scraped the hides, wove bark and grasses, made garments, made baskets, made pottery, made all

[82]

THE HOME AS A WORKSHOP

that was made for her own family, save the weapons of slaughter, now the thousand manufactures of a million mills supply our complex needs and pleasures. Where she tamed and herded a few beasts for her own family, now from ranchman to packer move the innumerable flocks and herds of the great plains; where she ploughed with a stick and reaped with a knife, for her own family, now gathered miles of corn cross continent and ocean to feed all nations. Where she prepared the food and reared the child for her own family—what! Has the world stopped? Is history a dream? Is social progress mere imagination?—*there she is yet!* Back of history, at the bottom of civilisation, untouched by a thousand whirling centuries, the primitive woman, in the primitive home, still toils at her primitive tasks.

All industries began at home, there is no doubt of that. All other industries have left home long ago. Why have these stayed? All other industries have grown. Why have not these?

What conditions, social and economic, what shadowy survival of oldest superstitions, what iron weight of custom, law, religion, can be adduced in explanation of such a paradox as this? Talk of Siberian mammoths handed down in ice, like some crystallised fruit of earliest ages! What are they compared with this antedeluvian

[83]

relic! By what art, what charm, what miracle, has the twentieth century preserved *alive* the prehistoric squaw!

This is a phenomenon well worth our study, a subject teeming with interest, one that concerns every human being most closely—most vitally. Sociology is beginning to teach us something of the processes by which man has moved up and on to his present grade, and may move farther. Among those processes none is clearer, simpler, easier to understand, than industrial evolution. Its laws are identical with those of physical evolution, a progression from the less to the greater, from the simple to the complex, a constant adaptation of means to ends, a tendency to minimise effort and maximise efficiency. The solitary savage applies his personal energy to his personal needs. The social group applies its collective energy to its collective needs. The savage works by himself, for himself; the civilised man works in elaborate inter-dependence with many, for many. By the division of labour and its increasing specialisation we vastly multiply skill and power; by the application of machinery we multiply the output; by the development of business methods we reduce expense and increase results; the whole line of growth is the same as that which makes a man more efficient in action than his weight in shellfish. He is more highly organised and specialised. So is modern industry.

The solitary savage knew neither specialisation nor organisation—he " did his own work." This process gives the maximum of effort and the minimum of results. Specialised and organised industry gives the minimum of effort and the maximum of results. That is civilised industry.

The so idealised and belauded " home industries " are still savage. The modern home is built and furnished by civilised methods. Arts, crafts, and manufactures, sciences, professions, many highly sublimated processes of modern life combine to make perfect the place where we live; but the industries practised in that place remain at the first round of the ladder.

Instead of having our pick of the latest and best workers, we are here confined to the two earliest—the Housewife and the Housemaid. The housewife is the very first, and she still predominates by so large a majority as to make us wonder at the noisy prominence of " the servant question." (It is not so wonderful, after all, for that class of the population which keeps servants is the class which makes the most noise. Even in rich America, even in richest New York, in *nine-tenths* of the families the housewife " does her own work." This is so large a proportion that we will consider the house-wife first—and fully.

Why was woman the first worker? Because she is a mother. All living animals are under the law of, first, self-preservation, and, second, race-preservation. But the second really comes first; the most imperative forces in nature compel the individual to sacrifice to the race. This law finds its best expression in what we call " the maternal sacrifice." Motherhood means giving. There is no limit to this urgency. The mother gives all she has to the young, including life. In many low organisms the sacrifice is instantaneous and complete—the mother dies in giving birth to the young—just lays her eggs and dies. Such forms of life have to remain low, how-ever. The defunct mothers can be of no further use to the young, so they have to be little instinctive automata, hopelessly arrested in the path of progress.

Nature perceived that this wholly sacrified mother was not the best kind. Little by little the usefulness of the mother was prolonged, the brooding mother, the feeding mother, lastly the nursing mother, highest of all. Order mammalia stands at the top, type of efficient motherhood.

When human development began, new paths were open to mother-love—new tasks to maternal energy. The human mother not only nursed and guarded the child, but exercised her dawning ingenuity in adding to its comfort by making things.

The constructive tendency is essentially feminine; the destructive masculine. Male energy tends to scatter and destroy, female to gather and construct. So human labour comes by nature from the woman, was hers entirely for countless ages, while the man could only hunt and fight, or prance and prophesy as " medicine man "; and this is still so in those races which remain savage. Even in so advanced a savage race as the Zulus, the women do the work; and our own country has plenty of similar examples near at hand.

As human civilisation is entirely dependent on progressive industry, while hunting and fighting are faculties we share with the whole carnivora, it is easy to see that during all those ages of savagery the woman was the leader. She represented the higher grade of life; and carried it far enough to bring to birth many of the great arts as well as the humbler ones, especially the invaluable art of language.*

But maternal energy has its limits. What those limits are may be best studied in an ant's nest or a beehive. These marvellous insects, perfected types of industry and of maternity, have succeeded in *organising motherhood.*

*See Otis Mason, " Woman's Share in Primitive Culture."

THE HOME

Most creatures reproduce individually, these collectively
—all personal life absolutely lost in the group life.
Moved by an instinct coincident with its existence, the
new-hatched ant, still weak and wet from the pupa, stag-
gers to the nearest yet unborn to care for it, and cares
for it devotedly to the end of life.

One bee group-mother, crawling from cell to cell, lays
eggs unnumbered for the common care; the other group-
mothers, their own egg-laying capacity in abeyance,
labour unceasingly in the interests of those cemmon eggs;
and the delicate perfection of provision and service thus
attained results in—what? In a marvellous motherhood
and a futile fatherhood; the predominant female, the almost negligible male—a temporary fertilising agent
merely; in infinite reproduction, and that is all; in more
bees, and more ants, more and more for ever, like the
sands of the sea. They would cover the earth like a
blanket but for merciful appetites of other creatures.
But this is only multiplication—not improvement. Nature has one more law to govern life besides self-preservation and reproduction—progress. To be, to re-be,
and to be better is the law. It is not enough to keep
one's self alive, it is not enough to keep one's kind alive,
we must improve. This law of growth, which is the
grand underlying one that moves the universe, acts on

living species mainly through the male. He is progressive where the female is conservative by nature. He is a variant where she is the race type. This tendency to vary is one of the most beneficent in nature. Through it comes change, and, through change, improvement. The unbridled flow of maternal energy is capable of producing an exquisite apparatus for child-rearing, and no more. The masculine energy is needed also, for the highest evolution.

Well is it for the human race that the male savage finally took hold of the female's industry. Whether he perceived her superiority and sought to emulate it is doubtful; more probably it was the pressure of economic conditions which slowly forced him to it. The glaring proofs of time taught him that the pasture was more profitable than the hunting ground, and the cornfield than the pasture. The accumulating riches produced by the woman's industry drew him on. Slowly, reluctantly, the lordly fighter condescended to follow the humble worker, who led him by thousands of years. In the hands of the male, industry developed. The woman is a patient, submissive, inexhaustible labourer. The pouring forces of maternity prompt her to work for ever— for her young. Not so the man. Working is with him an acquired habit, and acquired very late in his racial

[89]

life. The low-grade man still in his heart despises it, he still prefers to be waited on by women, he still feels most at home in hunting and fighting. And man alone being represented in the main fields of modern industry, this male instinct for hunting and fighting plays havoc with the true economic processes. He makes a warfare of business, he makes prey of his competitors, he still seeks to enslave—to make others work for him, instead of freely and joyously working all he can. The best industrial progress needs both elements—ours is but a compromise as yet, something between the beehive and the battlefield.

But, with all the faults of unbridled male energy, it has lifted industry from the limits of the home to that of the world. Through it has come our splendid growth; much marred by evils of force and fraud, crude, wasteful, cruel, but progressive; and infinitely beyond the level of these neglected rudimentary trades left at home; left to the too tender mercies of the housewife.

The iron limits of her efficiency are these: First, that of average capacity. Just consider what any human business would be in which there was no faintest possibility of choice, of exceptional ability, of division of labor. What would shoes be like if every man made his own, if the shoemaker had never come to his development? What

would houses be like if every man made his own? Or
hats, or books, or waggons? To confine any industry to
the level of a universal average is to strangle it in its
cradle. And there, for ever, lie the industries of the
housewife. What every man does alone for himself, no
man can ever do well—or woman either. That is the
first limit of the " housewife."

The next is the maternal character of this poor primeval labourer. Because of her wealth of power and patience it does not occur to her to make things easier for
herself. The fatal inertia of home industries lies in their
maternal basis. The work is only done for the family—
the family is satisfied—what remains? There is no other
ambition, no other incentive, no other reward. Where
the horizon of duty and aspiration closes down with
one's immediate blood relations, there is no room for
growth.

All that has pushed and pulled reluctant man up the
long path of social evolution has not touched the home-
bound woman. Whatever height he reached, her place
was still the same. The economic relation of the sexes
here works* with tremendous force. Depending on the
male for her economic profit, her own household labours
kept to the sex-basis, and never allowed to enter the open

* See " Women and Economics," C. P. Stetson.

[91]

market, there was nothing to modify her original sex-tendency to work with stationary contentment. If we can imagine for a moment a world like ours, with all our elaborate business processes in the hands of women, and the men still in the position of the male savage—painted braves, ready for the warpath, and good for little else—we get a comparison with this real condition, where the business processes are in the hands of men, and the women still in the position of the female savage—docile toilers for the family, and good for little else. That is the second limit of the housewife—that she is merely working for her own family—in the sex-relation—not the economic relation; as servant to the family instead of servant to the world.

Next comes her isolation. Even the bottom-level of a universal average—even the blind patience of a working mother—could be helped up a little under the beneficent influence of association. In the days when the ingenious squaw led the world, she had it. The women toiled together at their primitive tasks and talked together as they toiled. The women who founded the beginnings of agriculture were founders also of the village; and their feminine constructive tendencies held it together while the destructive tendencies of the belligerent male continually tore it apart. All through that

[92]

babyhood of civilisation, the hunting and fighting instinct made men prey upon the accumulated wealth resultant from the labouring instinct of women—but industry conquered, being the best. As industry developed, as riches increased, as property rights were defined, as religions grew, women were confined more and more closely at home. Later civilisations have let them out to play—but not to work. The parasitic female of the upper classes is allowed the empty freedom of association with her useless kind; but the housewife is still confined to the house.

We are now giving great attention to this matter of home industry. We are founding chairs of Household Science, we are writing books on Domestic Economics; we are striving mightily to elevate the standard of home industry—and we omit to notice that it is just because it is home industry that all this trouble is necessary.

So far as home industry had been affected by world industry, it has improved. The implements of cooking and cleaning, for instance—where should we be if our modern squaw had to make her own utensils, as did her ancient prototype? The man, in world industry, makes not only the house, with all its elaborate labour-saving and health-protecting devices; not only the furniture of the house, the ornaments, hangings, and decorations, but the implements of the home industries as well. Go to the household furnishing store of our day—remember the one pot of the savage family to boil the meat and wash the baby—and see the difference between " home-made " and " world-made " things.

So far as home industry has progressed, it is through contact with the moving world outside; so far as it remains undeveloped, it is through the inexorable limitations of the home in itself.

There is one more limitation to be considered—the number of occupations practised. Though man has taken out and developed all the great trades, and, indeed, all trades beyond a certain grade, he has left the roots of quite a number at home. The housewife practises the conflicting elements of many kinds of work. First, she is cook. Whatever else is done or undone, we must eat; and since eating is ordained to be done at home, that is her predominant trade. The preparation and service of food is a most useful function; and as a world-industry, in the hands of professionals, students, and experts, it has reached a comparatively high stage of development.

In the nine-tenths of our homes where the housewife is cook, it comes under all these limitations: First, average capacity; second, sex-tendency; third, isolation; fourth, conflicting duties.

The cook, having also the cleaning to do, the sewing, mending, nursing, and care of children, the amount of time given to cooking is perforce limited. But even the plainest of home cooking must take up a good proportion of the day. The cooking, service, and " cleaning up " of ordinary meals, in a farmhouse, with the contributary processes of picking, sorting, peeling, washing, etc., and the extra time given to special baking, pickling, and preserving, take fully six hours a day. To the man, who is out of the house during work-hours, and who seldom estimates woman's work at its real value, this may seem extreme, but the working housewife knows it is a fair allowance, even a modest one.

There are degrees of speed, skill, intelligence, and purchasing power, of course; but this is a modest average; two hours for breakfast, three for dinner, one for supper. The preparation of food as a household industry takes up half the working time of half the population of the world. This utterly undeveloped industry, inadequate and exhausting, takes nearly a quarter of a twelve-hour day of the world's working force.

Cooking and sewing are inimical; the sewing of the housewife is quite generally pushed over into the

[95]

evening as well as afternoon, thus lengthening her day considerably. Nursing, as applied to the sick, must come in when it happens, other things giving way at that time. Cleaning is continuous. Cooking, of course, makes cleaning; the two main elements of dirt in the household being grease and ashes; another, and omnipresent one, dust. Then, there are the children to clean, and the clothes to clean—this latter so considerable an item as to take two days of extra labour—during which, of course, other departments must be less attended.

We have the regular daily labour of serving meals and "clearing up," we have the regular daily labour of keeping the home in order; then we have the washing day, ironing day, baking day, and sweeping day. Some make a special mending day also. This division, best observed by the most competent, is a heroic monument to the undying efforts of the human worker to specialise. But we have left out one, and the most important one, of our home industries—the care of children.

Where is Children's Day?

The children are there every day, of course. Yes, but which hour of the day? With six for food, with—spreading out the washing and ironing over the week—two for laundry, with—spreading the sweeping day and adding the daily dusting and setting to rights—two for cleaning; and another two for sewing—after these twelve hours of necessary labour are accounted for, what time remains for the children?

The initial purpose of the home is the care of children. The initial purpose of motherhood is the care of children. How are the duties of the mother compatible with the duties of the housewife? How can child-culture, as a branch of human progress, rise to any degree of proficiency in this swarming heap of rudimentary trades?

Nothing is asked—here—as to how the housewife, doing all these things together her life long, can herself find time for culture and development; or how can she catch any glimmer of civic duty or public service beyond this towering pile of domestic duty and household service. The particular point herein advanced is that the conditions of home industry *as such* forever limit the growth of the industry so practised; forever limit the growth of the persons so practising them; and also tend to limit the growth of the society which is content to leave any of its essential functions in this distorted state.

Our efforts to " lift the standard of household industry " ignore the laws of industry. We seek by talking and writing, by poetising and sermonising, and playing on every tender sentiment and devout aspiration, to convince the housewife that there is something particularly exalted and beautiful, as well as useful, in her occupation. This shows our deep-rooted error of sex-distinction in industry. We consider the work of the woman in the house as essentially feminine, and fail to see that, as work, it is exactly like any other kind of human activity, having the same limitations and the same possibilities.

Suppose we change the sex and consider for a while the status of a house-husband. He could be a tall, strong, fine-looking person—man-servants often are. He could love his wife and his children—industrial status does not affect these primal instincts. He could toil from morning to night, manfully, to meet their needs.

Suppose we are visiting in such a family. We should find a very rude small hut—no one man could build much of a house, but, ah! the tender love, the pride, the intimate emotion he would put into that hut! For his heart's dearest—for his precious little ones—he had dragged together the fallen logs—chipped them smooth with his flint-ax (there could have been no metal work while every man was a house-husband), and piled them together. With patient, loving hands he had daubed the chinks with clay, made beds of leaves, hung hides upon the walls. Even some rude stools he might have contrived—though furniture really belongs to a later period. But over all comes the incessant demand for food. His cherished family must eat, often and often, and under that imperative necessity all others wait.

So he goes forth to the hunt, brave, subtle, fiercely ingenious; and, actuated by his ceaseless love for his family he performs wonders. He brings home the food —day after day—even sometimes enough for several days, though meat does not keep very long. The family would have food of a sort, shelter of a sort, and love. But try to point out to the house-husband what other things he could obtain for them, create for them, provide for them, if he learned to combine with other men, to exchange labour, to organise industry. See his virtuous horror!

What! Give up his duty to his family! Let another man hunt for them!—another man build their home— another man make their garments! He will not hear of it. "It is my duty as a husband," he will tell you, "to serve my wife. It is my duty as a father to serve my children. No other person could love them as I do, and ' without that love the work would not be done as well." Strong in this conviction, the house-husband would remain intrenched in his home, serving his family with might and main, having no time, no strength, no brain capacity for undertaking larger methods; and there he and his family would all be, immovable in the Stone Age.

Never was any such idiot on earth as this hypothetical home-husband. It was not in him to stay in such primitive restrictions. But he has been quite willing to leave his wife in that interestingly remote period.

The permanent error of the housewife lies-in that assumption that her love for her family makes her service satisfactory. Family affection has nothing to do with the specialist's skill; nor with the specialist's love of his work for the pleasure of doing it. That is the kind of love that makes good work; and that is the kind of work the world needs and the families within it. Men, specialised, give to their families all that we know of modern comforts, of scientific appliances, of works of art, of the complex necessities and conveniences of modern life. Women, unspecialised, refuse to benefit their families in like proportion; but offer to them only the grade of service which was proper enough in the Stone Age, but is a historic disgrace to-day.

A house does not need a wife any more than it does a husband. Are we never to have a man-wife? A really suitable and profitable companion for a man instead of the bond-slave of a house? There is nothing in the work of a house which requires marital or maternal affection. It does require highly developed skill and business sense—but these it fails to get.

Would any amount of love on the part of that inconceivable house-husband justify him in depriving his family of all the fruits of progress? What a colossal charge of malfeasance in office could be brought against such a husband—such a father; who, under the name of love, should so fail in his great first duty—Progress.

How does the woman escape this charge? Why is not she responsible for progress, too? By that strange assumption does she justify this refusal to keep step with the world? She will tell you, perhaps, that she cannot do more than she does—she has neither time nor strength nor ambition for any more work. So might the house-husband have defended himself—as honestly and as reasonably. It is true. While every man had to spend all his time providing for his own family, no man ever had, or ever could have, time, strength, or ambition to do more.

It is not *more* work that is asked of women, but less. It is *a different method* of work. Human progress rests upon the interchange of labour; upon work done humanly for each other, not, like the efforts of the savage or the brute, done only for one's own. The housewife, blinded by her ancient duty, fails in her modern duty.

It is true that, while she does this work in this way, she can do no more. Therefore she must stop doing it, and learn to do differently. The house will not be " neglected " by her so doing; but is even now most shamefully neglected by her antique methods of labour. The family will not be less loved because it has a skilled worker to love it. Love has to pass muster in results, as well as intentions. Here are five mothers, equally loving. One is a Hottentot. One is an Eskimo. One is a Hindoo. One is a German peasant woman. One is an American and a successful physician.

Which could do most for her children? All might compete on even terms if " love is enough," as poets have claimed; but *which could best provide for her children?*

Neither overflowing heart nor overburdened hand sufficiently counts in the uplifting of the race; that rests on *what is done.* The position of the housewife is a final limitation and a continuous, increasing injury both to the specific industries of the place, and to her first great duty of motherhood. The human race, fathered only by house-husbands, would never have moved at all. The human race, mothered only by housewives, has moved only half as fast and as far as it rightly should have done, and the work the patient housewife spends her life on is pitifully behind in the march of events. The home as a workshop is utterly insufficient to rightly serve the needs of the growing world.

VI

THE HOME AS A WORKSHOP

II. *The Housemaid*

AMONG that tenth part of the population sufficiently rich to keep servants, the conditions of domestic industry are familiar to us. This is the tenth which is most conscious, and most vocal. It has the widest range of social contact; it is most in touch with literature; both in speech and writing we hear oftenest from the small class who keep servants.

The woman who does her own work is not usually a writer and has little time for reading. Moreover, her difficulties, though great, are not of the sort that confound the mistress of servants. The housewife is held to her work by duty and by love; also by necessity. She cannot " better herself " by leaving; and indeed, without grave loss and pain, she cannot leave at all. So the housewife struggles on, too busy to complain; and accomplishes, under this threefold bond of duty, love, and necessity far more than can be expected of a comparatively free agent.

THE HOME AS A WORKSHOP

Therefore we hear little of the " problem " of domestic service where the wife is the servant; and have to draw our conclusions from such data as the large percentage of farmers' wives who become insane, and such generalisations as those of the preceding chapter. But the " Servant Question " is clearly before us. It is an economic problem which presses upon us all, (that tenth of us all which is so prominent that it tacitly assumes its problem to be universal;) and the pressure of which increases daily. We are even beginning to study it scientifically. Miss Salmon's valuable book on " Domestic Service " contributes much useful information. The Household Economic Association exists largely to alleviate the distresses of this system of industry. Scarce one women (of this tenth) but feels the pinch of our imperfect method of doing housework, and as they become better educated and more intelligent, as some of them even learn something of more advanced economic processes, this crude, expensive, and inadequate system causes more and more uneasiness and distress.

What is the status of household industry as practised by servants? It is this: The Housewife having become the Lady of the House, and the work still having to be done in the house, others must be induced to do it. In the period from which this custom dates it was a simple

[105]

matter of elevating " the wife or chief wife " * to a position of dominance, and leaving the work to be done by the rest of the women. Domestic service, as an industrial status, dates from the period of the polygynous group; the household with the male head and the group of serving women; from the time when wives were slaves and slaves were wives, indiscriminately. (See domestic relations of Jacob.)

The genesis of the relation being thus established, it is easy to account for its present peculiar and dominating condition—celibacy. The housemaid is the modern derivative from the slave-wife. She may no longer be the sub-wife of the master—but neither may she be another man's wife.

No married man wishes his wife to serve another man. This household service, being esteemed as a distinctly feminine function, closely involved with maternity, or at least with marriage, or, if not with marriage, at the very least with woman's devotion, and quite inconsistent with any other marriage; therefore we find the labours of the household performed by celibate women of a lower class. Our modern household is but a variation of the primitive group—the man and his serving women still.

In the period of slave labour, where both men and

* See Veblen's " Theory of the Leisure Class."

women were owned and exploited, we find household
labour performed by men; and in those Oriental nations
where slavery yet exists we find man-service common in
the home. Also in nations still influenced by feudalism,
where service once went with the soil, where the lord is
still attended by what was originally his contingent of
fighting men, but which has gradually dwindled to an
array of footmen and butlers; there we find men still
contented, or partially contented, to do house-service.
But it ranks last and lowest in man's mind, and justly.
As fast as industrial evolution progresses we find men
less and less content to do this work in this way; or, for
that matter, women either.

In the highly advanced economic status of America we
are especially confronted with this difficulty, and have
to supply our needs from nations still largely under the
influence of the feudal régime, or those in the yet lower
period of slavery. Men-servants, when obtained, are
generally satisfactory; no public outcry is made over
them. It is the " servant-girl " that constitutes the
element of difficulty, and it is she that we must consider.

Let it be clearly held in mind that the very first
economic relation was that of sex, based on the natural
tendency of the female to work; sex-labour. The second

stage of economic relation is that of force; slave-labour. The next is that of payment, what we call the contract system; wage-labour.

Social evolution still shows us all these forms actively present in this age, though belonging to such remote and different ones; just as physical evolution still shows us monad and mollusk as well as vertebrate mammals. Each stage has its use and value. But when an early stage comes into contact with a later one there is trouble.

We have all seen how inevitably a savage status recedes and disappears before the civilised. Individual savages may be assimilated by the civilised competing race; but savagery and civilisation cannot coexist when they come in contact and competition. A savage cult may endure on an island in the South Seas, but not in England or America. So an early status of labour has to give way to a later; as shown so conspicuously in the last great historic instance in our own country.

Household industry is a mixed status, composed mainly of sex-labour, the first stage; and partially of slave-labour, the second. This slave-labour is in the act of changing to contract labour; and, as such, cannot endure the conditions of home industry. The housewife has to, the house-slave had to, the house-servant mostly had to;

but the house-*employee* does not have to, and will not if she can help it.

The contract status of labour is incompatible with home industry. Note how the condition of celibacy intereacts upon the relation. We expect of our house-servants that they be " attached," " loyal," " faithful," " respectful," " devoted "; we do not say they always are, but that is our ideal; these are the qualities for which we most praise them. Attachment is especially valued. If only we could still *own* them! Then there would be that pleasant sense of permanence and security so painfully lacking in our modern house-service. Short of owning them we seek by various futile methods to " attach " them. Some societies give medals for long service. The best thing we can say of a servant is " she stayed with me for seven years! " or whatever period we can boast. Now we do not seek to " attach " our butcher or baker or candlestick-maker; why our cook? Because this status of celibacy has necessarily resulted in the most painful conditions of transient incapacity in house-service.

People must marry. People ought to marry. People will marry, whether we say yes or no. Why should the housemaid stay a maid for our sakes? What do we offer in the exciting prospect of always doing the same work for the same wages, compared to the prospect of doing the same work, without wages, it is true, but with a " mechanic's lien " on her husband's purse? Or what would any scale of wages or promotion be against the joys of a home of her own, a husband of her own, children of her own?

We, intrenched in our own homes and families, think she ought to be satisfied with serving our husbands and children, but she is not—and never will be. There is of course a certain percentage of old maids and widows, sufficiently disagreeable not to be wanted by their relatives, or sufficiently independent not to want them; sufficiently capable to hold a place as house-servant, but not sufficiently capable to follow any other trade; or, in last possibility, there is here and there that Blessed Damosel of our domestic dreams—a strong, capable, ingenious woman, not hampered by any personal ties or affections; not choosing to marry; preferring to work in a kitchen to working in a shop; and so impressed by the august virtues and supreme importance of our family that she becomes " attached " to it for life. These cases are, however, rare. In the vast majority of households the maid is a maid, a young woman of the lower classes, doing this work because she can do no other, and doing it only until she marries. The resultant conditions of the industry so practised are precisely what we might expect.

This young woman is in no way attached to the family. A family is connected by the ties of sex, by marriage and heredity, with occasional cases of adoption. If the servant is not a relative, or adopted, she does not belong to the family. She has left her father's family, and looks forward to her husband's, meanwhile as an aid to the first or a means to the latter, she serves ours. She is of the lower classes because no others will do this work. She is ignorant because, if she were intelligent, she would not do it—does not do it; the well-schooled, well-trained young woman much prefers other work. So we find household industry in that tenth of our homes not served by the housewife, is in the hands of ignorant and inferior young women, *under conditions of constant change.*

The position of the lady of the house, as this procession of untrained, half-trained, ill-trained, or at least *otherwise*-trained young women march through her domain, is like that of the sergeant of companies of raw recruits. She " lifts 'em—lifts 'em—lifts 'em "—but there is never any " charge that wins the day."

Household industry we must constantly remember never rises to the level of a regular trade. It is service—

not " skilled labour." What is done there is done under no broad light of public improvement, but is merely catering to the personal tastes and habits, whims and fancies of one family. The lady of the house is by no means a captain of industry. She is not a trainer and governor of able subordinates, like the mate of a ship or the manager of a hotel. Her position is not one of power, but of helplessness. She has to be done for and waited on. Whatever maternal instinct may achieve at first hand in the woman-who-does-her-own-work, it does *not* make competent instructors. When the lady of the house's husband gets rich enough she hires a house-keeper to engage, discharge, train, and manage the housemaids.

Here and there we do find an efficient lady of the house who can do wonders even with this stream of transient incapacity, but the prominence of the servant-question proves her rarity. If all ladies of houses could bring order out of such chaos, could meet constant needs by transient means, the subtleties of refined tastes by the inefficiencies of unskilled labour, then nothing more need be said. But the thing cannot be done. The average house-mistress is not a servant-charmer and the average housemaid is *necessarily incapable.* This is what should be squarely faced and acknowledged. The kind of work that needs to be done to keep a modern home healthy, comfortable, and refined, cannot be done—can never be done—by this office-boy grade of labour. Because home industry *is* home industry, because it has been left aborted in the darkness of private life while other industries have grown so broad and high in the light of public life, we have utterly failed to recognise its true value.

These industries, so long neglected and misused, are of supreme importance. The two main ones—the preparation of food and the care of children—can hardly be overestimated in value to the race. On the one the health of the world mainly depends, yes, its very life. On the other the progress of the world depends, and that is more than life. That these two great social functions should be left contentedly to the hands of *absolutely the lowest grade of labour in our civilisation* is astounding. It is the lowest grade of labour not because it is performed by the lowest class of labour—humanity can grow to splendid heights from that beginning, and does so every day; but it is the lowest because it is carried on in the home.

The conditions of home industry as practised by either housewife or housemaid are hopelessly restrictive. They are, as we have seen, the low standard of average

[113]

capacity; the element of sex tendency; the isolation and the unspecialised nature of the work. In two of these conditions the housemaid gains on the housewife. She is partly out of the sex-tendency status and partly into the contract relation; hence the patient, submissive, conservative influence is lightened. In families of greater affluence there is some specialisation; we have varieties in housemaid; cookmaid, scullerymaid, nursemaid, chambermaid, parlourmaid, lady'smaid—as many as we can afford; and in such families we find such elevation of home-industry as is possible; marred, however, by serious limitations.

Household industry is a world question; and in no way to be answered by a solution only possible of application to one family in a thousand. It is a question of our time and the future, and not met by a solution which consists in maintaining an elaborate archaism. The proper feeding of the world to-day is no more to be guaranteed by one millionaire's French cook, than was the health of the Roman world by one patrician's Greek doctor.

Human needs, in remote low stages of social development, were met by privately owned labourers. As late as the Middle Ages the great lord had in his *menie* every kind of functionary to minister to his wants; not only his private servants of the modern kind, with butlers and sutlers and pantlers in every degree; but his armourer, his tailor, his minstrel, and his fool.

The feudal lord kept a fool to amuse him, whereas we go to the theatre. He kept a cook to feed him—and we do it yet. He kept a poet to celebrate his deeds and touch his emotions. We have made poetry the highest class in literature, and literature the world's widest art—by setting the poet free.

To work for the world at large is necessary to the development of the work. A private poet is necessarily ignoble. So is a private cook. The iron limitations of household service are immutable—world service has none. To cater to the whims of one master lowers both parties concerned. To study the needs of humanity and minister to them is the line of social progress.

There is nothing private and special in the preparation of food; a more general human necessity does not exist. There must be freedom and personal choice in the food prepared, but it no more has to be cooked for you than the books you love best have to be written for you. We flatter ourselves that we get what we want by having it done at home. Apply that condition to any other kind of human product and see if it holds. We get what we want by free choice from the world's markets—not from

a workshop in the back yard. Imagine the grade of
production, the arts, crafts, and manufactures, that we
should have to select from, if we tried to have all things
made for us by private servants! Apply the intelligence
and skill of this zoetrope procession of housemaids to
watch-making or shoe-making, or umbrella-making, or
the making of paper, or glass, or steel, or any civilised
commodity; and if we can easily see how immeasurably
incompetent these flitting handmaids would be for any
of these lines of work, why do we imagine them competent
to prepare food and take care of children? Because we
have never thought of it at all.

Men are too busy doing other things, too blinded by
their scorn for " women's work." Women are too busy
doing these things to think about them at all; or if they
think, stung by the pain of pressing inconvenience, they
only think personally, they only feel it for themselves,
each one blindly buried in her own home, like the crafty
ostrich with his head in the sand.

The question is a public one; none could be more so.
It affects in one of its two branches every human being
except those who board; every home, without exception.
Perhaps some impression may be made on the blank
spaces of our untouched minds by exhibiting the
economic status of home industry.

THE HOME AS A WORKSHOP

We Americans are credited with acuteness and good business sense. How can we reconcile ourselves to the continuance of a system not only so shamefully inadequate, but so ruinously expensive? If we are not mortified to find that our boasted industrial progress carries embedded in its very centre this stronghold of hoary antiquity, this knotted, stumpy bunch of amputated rudiments; if we are not moved by the low standard of general health as affected by food, and the *no* standard of general education as affecting the baby, perhaps we can be stimulated somewhat by the consideration of expense.

The performance of domestic industries involves, first, an enormous waste of labour. The fact that in nine cases out of ten this labour is unpaid does not alter its wastefulness. If half the men in the world stayed at home to wait on the other half, the loss in productive labour would be that between half and the fraction required to do the work under advanced conditions, say one-twentieth. Any group of men requiring to be cooked for, as a ship's crew, a lumber camp, a company of soldiers, have a proportionate number of cooks. To give each man a private cook would reduce the working strength materially. Our private cooks being women makes no difference in the economic law. We are so accustomed to rate women's labour on a sex-basis, as being her "duty" and not justly commanding any return, that we have quite overlooked this tremendous loss of productive labour.

Then there is the waste of endless repetition of "plant." We pay rent for twenty kitchens where one kitchen would do. All that part of our houses which is devoted to these industries, kitchen, pantry, laundry, servants' rooms, etc., could be eliminated from the expense account by the transference of the labour involved to a suitable workshop. Not only our rent bills, but our furnishing bills, feel the weight of this expense. We have to pay severally for all these stoves and dishes, tools and utensils, which, if properly supplied in one proper place instead of twenty, would cost far less to begin with; and, in the hands of skilled professionals, would not be under the tremendous charge for breakage and ruinous misuse which now weighs heavily on the householder. Then there is the waste in fuel for these nineteen unnecessary kitchens, and lastly and largest of any item except labour, the waste in food.

First the waste in purchasing in the smallest retail quantities; then the waste involved in separate catering, the "left overs" which the ingenious housewife spends her life in trying to "use up"; and also the waste caused by carelessness and ignorance in a great majority

of cases. Perhaps this last element, careless ignorance, ought to cover both waste and breakage, and be
counted by itself, or as a large item in the labour account.

Count as you will, there could hardly be devised a more
wasteful way of doing necessary work than this domestic
way. It costs on the most modest computation three
times what it need cost. Once properly aroused to a
consideration of these facts it will be strange indeed if
America's business sense cannot work out some system of
meeting these common human necessities more effectually
and more economically.

The housemaid would be more of a step in advance if
the housewife, released from her former duties, then
entered the ranks of productive labour, paid her substitute, and contributed something further to the world's
wealth. But nothing could be farther from the thoughts
of the Lady of the House. Her husband being able to
keep more than one woman to do the work of the house ;
and much preferring to exhibit an idle wife, as proof of
his financial position,* the idle wife proceeds so to conduct her house as to add to its labours most considerably.
The housewife's system of housekeeping is perforce
limited to her own powers. The size of the home, the

* See Veblen again.

nature of its furnishings and decorations, the kind of clothes worn by the women and children, the amount of food served and the manner of its service; all these are regulated by the housewife's capacity for labour. But once the housemaid enters the field of domestic labour there is a scale of increase in that labour which has no limits but the paying capacity of the man.

This element of waste cannot be measured, because it is a progressive tendency, it " grows by what it feeds upon " (as most things do, by the way!) and waxes greater and greater with each turn of the wheel. If the lady of the house, with one servant, were content to live exactly as she did before; keeping the work within the powers of the deputy, she would be simply and absolutely idle, and that is a very wearing condition; especially to woman, the born worker. So the lady of the house, mingling with other ladies of houses, none of them having anything but houses to play with, proceeds so to furnish, decorate, and arrange those houses, and so to elaborate the functions thereof, as to call for more and ever more housemaids to do the endless work.

This open door of senseless extravagance hinges directly upon the idle wife. She leaves her position of domestic service, not to take a higher one in world service;

but to depute her own work to an inferior and do none at all.

Thus we find that in the grade of household labour done by the housewife we have all those elements of incapacity and waste before explained; and that in the grade done by the housemaid we have a decrease in ability, a measurable increase in direct waste, and an immeasurable increase in the constantly rising sum of waste due to these bloated buildings stuffed with a thousand superfluities wherein the priceless energies of women are poured out in endless foolishness; in work that meets no real need; and in play that neither rests nor refreshes.

So far our sufferings under the present rapid elimination of the housemaid have taught us little. Our principal idea of bettering the condition is by training servants. We seriously propose to establish schools to train these reluctant young women to our service; even in some cases to pay them for going there. This is indeed necessary; for why should they pay for tuition, or even waste time in gratuitously studying, when they can get wages without?

We do not, and cannot, offer such graded and progressive salaries as shall tempt really high-class labour into this field. Skilled labour and domestic service are incompatible. The degree of intelligence, talent, learning, and trained skill which should be devoted to feeding and cleaning the human race will never consent to domestic service. It is the grade of work which forever limits its development, the place, the form of service. So long as the home is the workshop the housewife cannot, and the housemaid will not, even if she could, properly do this work for the neglected world.

Is it not time that the home be freed from these industries so palpably out of place? That the expense of living be decreased by two-thirds and the productive labour increased by nine-twentieths? That our women cease to be an almost universal class of house-servants; plus a small class of parasitic idlers and greedy consumers of wealth? That the preparation of food be raised from its present condition of inadequacy, injury, and waste to such a professional and scientific position that we may learn to spare from our street corners both the drug-store and the saloon? That the care of children become at last what it should be—the noblest and most valuable profession, to the endless profit of our little ones and progress of the race? And that our homes, no longer greasy, dusty workshops, but centres of rest and peace; no longer gorgeous places of entertainment that does not entertain, but quiet places of happiness; no longer costing the laborious lives of over-worked women or supporting the useless lives of idle ones, but properly maintained by organised industries; become enjoyed by men and women alike, both glad and honourable workers in an easy world?

VII

HOME-COOKING

WE are all reared in a traditional belief that what we get to eat at home is, by virtue of that location, better than what we get to eat anywhere else. The expression, "home-cooking," carries a connotation of assured excellence, and the popular eating-house advertises "pies like those your mother used to make," as if pie-making were a maternal function. Economy, comfort, and health are supposed to accompany our domestic food supply, and danger to follow the footsteps of those who eat in a hotel, a restaurant, or a boarding house. Is this long-accepted theory correct? Is the home, as the last stage of our elaborate processes of social nutrition, a success?

"Home-cooking" is an alluring phrase, but lay aside the allurement; the term applies to Eskimo hut, to Choctaw wigwam, to Turk and Chinaman and Russian Jew— whose home-cooking are we praising? Our own, of course. Which means nothing—absolutely nothing— but that the stomach adapts itself to what it has to live on—unless it is too poisonous. Of course we like what we are used to; be it sauerkraut or saleratus biscuit. We like tobacco too, and alcohol, and chloral and morphine.

The long-suffering human system (perhaps toughened by ages of home-cooking)—will adapt itself even to slow death.

But how does our universally praised home-cooking affect our health? To find it pure and undefiled, far from the deleterious products of mere business cooking, we must go to the isolated farmhouse. Does either the physician or the epicure point with pride to that dietary?

Its results are not due to lack of proper materials. There you have no much-blamed " baker's bread "; no " city milk "; no wilted vegetables and questionable meats; no painted confectionery and bakeshop sweets; no wild hurry to catch the morning car. You have mother love and mother instinct untrammelled, with the best materials we know, pure dairy produce and fresh vegetables and fruits. As a result, you should look for splendid health, clear complexions, bright eyes, perfect teeth, and sublime digestions. Instead, we find men who keep fairly well to middle life because their vigorous out-of-door work enables them to cope for a while with their home-cooking; but in the women you find a sadly low average of health and beauty. Dyspepsia is the rule. False teeth are needed before they are thirty.

THE HOME

Patent medicine is the family divinity. Their ordinary home-cooking is pork and potatoes; and their extraordinary home-cooking is such elaborate elegance of pie and cake as to supply every element of mischief omitted in the regular diet. The morbid appetites, the uneasy demand for stimulants, both in men and women, the rarity of good digestion—these do not prove much in favour of this system of preparing food.

The derivation of the habit is clear enough and easily traced. Among individual animals, the nutritive processes are simple. By personal effort each creature helps himself from a free supply, competing mercilessly with every other creature that comes in his way. Vegetarian animals compete peaceably as philosophical anarchists; carnivorous ones compete with more violence. Among both classes we find homes among those whose food is portable; holes, caves, or nests; places where the young can be guarded and their food brought to them. From the grisly heap of bones in the lion's den, or shells below the squirrel's nest, through the " kitchen middens " of primitive man, to the daily output of garbage from our well-loved homes to-day is an unbroken line. " A place to feed the young " was once a sufficient definition of a home, but the home has grown since then. Man is a social animal. He is part of something; his life is not dependent on his own efforts solely, but on those of many other men. We get our food, not by going out to quarrel with one another over a free supply, but by helping one another in various elaborate processes of production, distribution, and preparation. In this last process of preparation women long held a monopoly; and, as women were kept at home, so food was, naturally, prepared at home. But as soon as men banded together to go on long expeditions without women—which was at the beginning of the history of war—they learned to cook and eat away from home, and the cook, as a craftsman, was developed. This social functionary has been officiating for a long time. He has cooked as a business, giving his whole time to it; he has cooked for miscellaneous numbers, and has had to study averages; he has cooked for great dignitaries, epicurean and capricious. So, in course of time, has grown among us some little knowledge of the art and science of cooking. This growth has not taken place in the home. An ignorant overworked poor woman, cooking for her family, has not, and never can have, the time, means, or opportunity for the large experiment and practice which have given us the great diet-list of to-day. Each woman, learning only from her mother, has been able only to hand down to us the habits of a dark, untutored past.

THE HOME

Outside the home, man, the specialised cook, acting under pressure of larger needs and general competition, has gradually improved the vessels, utensils, and materials of the home food supply.

Note carefully that, in home-cooking, there are absent these great necessities of progress—specialisation and competition, as well as the wide practical experience which is almost as essential. Go among the most backward peasantry of any country and compare the " home-cooking " of each nation in its present form, with the specialised cooking of the best hotels, clubs, or of those great official or private entertainments which employ the professional cook. It is rare, of course, to find home-cooking wholly unaffected by social cooking, for man, as an ultra-domestic character, learns something elsewhere and brings it home ; but the point to be insisted on is that the development in cooking comes from outside the home, and does not originate in it. Still, in spite of all our progress, the great mass of mankind eats two meals at home ; women and children, three.

The preparation of food is still the main business of housekeeping ; its labour, the one great labour of the place ; its cost, the main expense. In building, the conveniences for this trade—kitchen, dining-room, pantry, cupboard, and cellar—require a large part of the outlay, and the furnishing of these with linen, china, and silver, as well as the wooden and iron articles, adds heavily to the list. The wife and mother still has, for her main duty, the management of the family food supply, even if she is not the principal worker, and the maintenance of domestic service, to keep our food system in motion, is one of the chief difficulties of modern life. Nine-tenths of our women " do their own work," as has been before shown. Those nine-tenths of the female population— as well as the majority of servants—expend most of their labour in the preparation of food and the cleansing processes connected with it.

With all this time, labour, and expense given to the feeding of humanity, what are the results? How are we educated in knowledge and taste as to right eating? What are our general food habits? To these questions it may be promptly answered that no other animal is so depraved in its feeding habits as man; no other animal has so many diseases of the alimentary system. The dog ranks next to us in diseases, and shares our home-cooking. The hog, which we most highly recommend, is " corn-fed," not reared on our remnants of the table. The long and arduous labours of public-spirited men have lifted our standards of living in many ways. Public sanitation, beginning outside and slowly driven in on the reluctant home, has lowered our death rate in the great filth-diseases which used to decimate the world. But the food diseases are not lessened. Wrong eating and wrong drinking are responsible for an enormous proportion of our diseases and our crimes, to say nothing of the still larger average of unhealthiness and unhappiness in which we live. Can we get at the causes of this department of human trouble? and, when found, do they bear any relation to our beloved custom of home-cooking and home-eating? We can—and they do. The trouble springs from two main features: bad food—insufficient, oversufficient, ill-chosen, or ill-prepared; and our own ignorance and lack of self-control.

Consider the bad food first. Food is produced all over the earth, passes through many hands, and is finally selected by the housewife. She is not a trained expert, and can never be while she confines herself to serving one house. She does not handle quantities sufficient or cater for consumers enough to gain large knowledge of her business. She is, in nine cases out of ten, limited financially in her buying power. These conditions make the food market particularly open to adulteration, and to the offering of inferior materials. The individual housewife cannot herself discriminate in all the subtleties of adulterated food, nor has she the time or the means to secure expert tests of her supplies. Moreover, her separate purchasing power is so small that it cannot intimidate the seller; he has ignorance and a small purse to deal with, and he deals with them accordingly.

The purchase of food in quantities by trained buyers would lift the grade of our supplies at once. No man is going to waste time and money in adulteration subject to daily analysis, or in offering stale, inferior articles which will not appear saleable to the trained eye. The wholesale poisoning of babies by bad milk is an evil our city governments are seeking to combat, but the helpless anarchy of a million ignorant homes, unorganised, untrained, and obliged to get the milk at once, renders our governmental efforts almost vain. Insufficient food is owing, in part, to economic causes, and in part to ignorance of what the body needs. On the economic side comes in a most important view of the home as a food purveyer. The private purchase and preparation of food is the most expensive method. It is wonderful to see how people cling to their notion of " the economy " of home-cooking. By the simplest business laws, of world-wide application, the small purchaser has to pay the largest price. The expenses incident to the re-retailing of f(od, from the apples rotting on the ground in New York State to the apples we purchase at twenty cents a quart for New York City tables, form a large part of the cost of living. Thousands of middlemen thrive like leeches on the long, slow current of food material, as it pours in myriad dribbling streams from the great sources of production, far away, into our innumerable kitchen doors.

In a city block there are, let us say, two hundred families, which, at our usual average of five individuals to a family, would number one thousand persons. The thousand persons should consume, we will say, five hundred quarts of milk a day. The purchase of five hundred quarts of milk and the proportionate cream, as well as butter, would maintain a nice little dairy—several blocks together would maintain a large one. Your bustling restaurant proudly advertises " Milk and cream fresh every day from our own dairies! " But your beloved home has no such purchasing power, but meekly absorbs pale cultures of tuberculosis and typhoid fever at eight cents a quart. The poorer people are, the more they pay for food, separately. The organised purchasing power of these same people would double their food supply, and treble it.

Besides the expense entailed in purchasing is that of private preparation. First, the " plant " is provided. For our two hundred families there are two hundred stoves, with their utensils. The kitchen, and all that it contains, with dining-rooms, etc., have been already referred to, but should be held firmly in mind as a large item in rent and furnishing. Next, there is the labour. Two hundred women are employed for about six hours a day each,—twelve hundred working hours,—at twenty cents an hour. This means two hundred and forty dollars a day, or sixteen hundred and eighty dollars a week, that the block of families is paying to have its wastefully home-purchased food more wastefully home-cooked. Of course, if these cooks are the housewives, they do not get the money; but the point is, that this much labour is *worth* that amount of money, and that productive energy is being wasted. What ought it to cost? One trained cook can cook for thirty, easily; three, more easily, for a hundred. The thousand people mentioned need, in largest allowance, thirty cooks—and the thirty cooks, organised, would not need six hours a day to do the same work, either. Thirty cooks, even at ten dollars a week, would be but three hundred dollars, and that is some slight saving as against sixteen hundred and eighty!

We have not mentioned fully another serious evil. " Insufficient food " would be easily removable from our list by a more economical method of buying and cooking it. The other element of insufficiency—ignorance,—would go also, if we had skilful and learned cooks and caterers instead of unskilled and unlearned amateurs, who know only how to cater to the demands of hungry children and injudicious men at home. Wise temperance workers know that many men drink because they are not properly fed; and women, too, consume tea and coffee to make up in stimulants for the lack of nutrition about which they know nothing. Under this same head comes the rest of that list, the over-sufficient, ill-chosen, and ill-prepared food. It is not simply that the two hundred amateur cooks (whether they be permanent wife or transient servant, they are all, in a business sense, amateurs,—ask a real cook!) waste money by their sporadic efforts, but their incapacity wastes our blood in our veins. We do not die, swift and screaming, from some sharp poison administered through malice; but our poor stomachs are slowly fretted by grease-hardened particles, and wearied out by heavy doses of hot dough. Only iron vigour can survive such things.

" It is ill-chosen," is one charge against home-cooking. What governs our choice? Why does a German eat decaying cabbage and mite-infested cheese, an American revel in fat-soaked steak and griddle-cakes, a Frenchman disguise questionable meats with subtly-blended spices, and so on, through the tastes of all the nations and localities? It is environment and heredity that governs us—that's all. It is not knowledge, not culture and experience, not an enlightened taste, or the real choice of a trained mind capable of choosing.

A child is fed by his mother, who transmits remote ancestral customs, unchanged by time. Children are hungry and like to eat. The young stomach is adapted to its food supply; it grows accustomed to it and " likes " it,—and the man continues to demand the doughnuts, the sauerkraut, the saleratus biscuit, which he " likes." One ghastly exception should be taken to this smooth statement. I have said that " the young stomach is adapted to its food supply." Alas, alas! This is true of those who survive; but think of the buried babies,—of the dear, dead children, of the " diseases incidental to childhood,"—and question if some part of that awful death-list is not due to our criminal ignorance of what is proper food! There is no knowledge, save the filtering down of ancient customs and what the private cook can pick up from house to house; no experience, save that gained by practising on one's own family or the family of one's employer—and I never heard of either wife or servant gathering statistics as to who lived and who died under her cooking—no special training; and no room or time or means to learn! It would be a miracle if all should survive.

The ignorance which keeps us so ill-fed *is an essential condition of home-cooking.* If we had only home-shoe-making, or home-doctoring, or home-tailoring—barbering—what you please—we should show the same wide-spread ignorance and lack of taste. What we have learned in cooking comes from the advance of that great branch of human industry in its free social field, and that advance has reacted to some degree on the immovable home.

Next consider self-control, the lack of which is so large a factor in our food diseases. We have attained some refinement of feeling in painting, music, and other arts; why are we still so frankly barbaric in our attitude toward food? Why does modern man, civilised, educated, cultured, still keep his body in a loathsome condition, still suffer, weaken, and die, from foul food habits? It is not alone the huge evil of intemperance in drink, or simple gluttony; but the common habits of our young girls, serenely indulging in unlimited candy, with its attendant internal consequences; or of our cultured women, providing at their entertainments a gross accumulation of unwholesome delicacies, with scarcely more discrimination than was shown by Heliogabalus.

[136]

HOME-COOKING

We eat what we like, and our liking is most crude and low.

The position of the woman who feeds us—the wife and mother—is responsible for this arrest of development. She is not a free cook, a trained cook, a scientific cook; she belongs to the family. She must cook for the man because he pays for it. He maintains the home—and her—largely for that very purpose. It is his home, his table, his market bill; and, if John does not like onions, or pork, or cereals, they do not appear. If Mrs. Peterkin paid for it, and John was cook, why John would cook to please her! In two ways is Mrs. Peterkin forced to cater to John's appetite; by this plain, economic fact, that it is his food she is cooking, and by the sexuo-economic fact that " the way to a man's heart is through his stomach." For profit and for love—to do her duty and to gain her ends—in all ways, the home cook is forced to do her home cooking to please John. It is no wonder John clings so ardently to the custom. Never again on earth will he have a whole live private cook to himself, to consider, before anything else, his special tastes and preferences. He will get better food, and he will have to get used to it. His tastes will be elevated by the quality of the food, instead of the quality of the food being adapted solely to his tastes. To the children, again, the mother caters under direct pressure of personal affection. It is very, very hard to resist the daily, yea, tri-daily, demands of those we love.

It is this steady, alluring effort of subservient love which keeps us still so primitively self-indulgent in our food habits. The mother-love of a dumb animal may teach her what is right for her young to eat, but it does not teach the human mother. Ask any doctor, any trained nurse, anyone who has watched the children of the poor. If the children of the rich are more wisely fed, it is not because of any greater amount of mother-love, but of some degree of mother-education. Motherhood and wifehood do not teach cooking.

What we need in our system of feeding the world is not instinct, affection, and duty, but knowledge, practice, and business methods. Those who are fitted by natural skill and liking to be cooks should cook, and many should profit by their improved products. Scientific training, free from the tender pressure of home habits, would soon eliminate our worst viands; and, from the wide choice offered by a general field of patronage, there would appear in time a cultivated taste. Greater freedom for personal idiosyncrasy would be given in this general field of choice, yet a simpler average would undoubtedly be formed. Great literature and great music were never developed when the bard performed for his master only.

We, keeping our food system still on this miserable basis of private catering to appetite, are thereby prevented from studying it with a view to race improvement. The discoveries of the food specialist and scientific dietist are lost in the dark recesses of a million homes, in the futile, half-hearted efforts of unskilled labour. What the immediate family " likes " is the governing law; no matter how wise may be the purpose of the mother-cook. With most of us food is scarcely thought of in its real main use—to supply bodily waste with judiciously combined materials.

The home-bred appetite cries out for " mother's cooking," with no more idea of its nutritive values than has a child. This is most remarkable among our enormous farming population, yet there most absolutely the case. The mechanic or business man has no dealings whatever with his food except to eat it. He gives over his life's health, his daily strength, into the hands of his beloved female domestic; and asks nothing whatever of her production except that it " taste good."

But the farmer has a different trade. With him the whole business of his life is to feed things that they may grow. He has to replenish the soil with the elements his crops exhaust, in order to reap the best crops, the most profit. And even more directly with his live-stock; from hen to horse, with pigs, sheep, and cattle, he has constantly to consider what to put into them in order to be sure of the product, not too much grain for the horse, not too much hay; enough " green feed " in season; the value of the silo, the amount of salt necessary; the effect of beets, of wild onions, in the grass and in the butter; what to give hens in winter to make them lay; how to regulate the diet for more milk and less cream, or for less milk and more cream; how to fatten, how to strengthen, how to improve—in all ways the farmer has to realise the importance of food values in his business.

Yet that same man, day after day, consumes his own food and sees his children fed, to say nothing of the mother of his children, without ever giving one thought to the nutritive values of that food. There must be enough to satisfy hunger, and it must " taste good," according to his particular brand of ancestry, his race habits, and early environment; but, beyond that, nothing is required.

The farmer has assistance in his business. He shares in the accumulated experience of many farmers, before him and about him. There are valuable experiments being made in his behalf by the Bureau of Agriculture.

He has trade papers to bring him the fruits of the world's progress in this line. Agriculture is one of the world's great functions, and has made magnificent progress. But humaniculture has no Bureau, no Secretary, no Experiment Stations; unless we count the recent experiments in boric-acid diet. The most valuable livestock on earth are casually fed by the haphazard efforts of any and every kind of ignorant woman; hired servants or married servants, as the case may be; dull, shortsighted, overworked women, far too busy in " doing the cooking " ever to study the science of feeding humanity. No science could ever make progress in such hands. Science must rest on broad observation, on the widest generalisation and deduction, on careful experiment and reconsideration.

This is forever impossible at home. Until the food laboratory entirely supersedes the kitchen there can be no growth. Many of us, struggling to sit fast between two stools, seeing the imperative need of scientific feeding for humanity, yet blindly clinging to the separate wife-mother-cook functionary, exhort " the woman " to study all this matter, and cheerfully to devote her life to scientifically feeding her beloved family.

" The woman "—that is, a woman, any woman, every woman, and that means the deadly Average, the hopelessly Isolated, the handicapped Maternal, with the Lack of Specialisation, the Confusion of other Trades, and the Lack of Incentive. Not until " The woman " in " the home " can everywhere manifest a high degree of skill as a doctor, as an architect, as a barber, as anything, can she manifest that high degree as a cook.

Cooking is an art; cooking is a science; cooking is a handicraft; cooking is a business. None of these can ever grow without following the laws of all industrial progress—specialisation, contact and exchange, legitimate competition, and the stimulus of large world-incentives. When we have these we shall be able to improve our kind of animal as much as we do other kinds. We cannot arbitrarily by breeding, but we can by nutrition and education—to an unknown extent. Nutrition, properly adjusted, nutrition for the human animal, has hardly been thought of by the home cook. The inexorable limit of our Home-cooking is the Home.

VIII

DOMESTIC ART

ONE of the undying efforts of our lives, of the lives of half the world, is " to make home beautiful." We love beauty, we love home, we naturally wish to combine the two. The rich spare no expense, the æsthetic no care and pains, in this continuous attempt; and the " home " papers, or " home departments " in other papers, teem with instruction on the subject for the eager, but untutored many.

In varying fields of work there is a strong current of improvement, in household construction, furnishing, and decoration; and new employments continually appear wherein the more cultured few apply their talents to the selection and arrangement of " artistic interiors " ready-made for the purchaser. Whole magazines are devoted to this end, articles unnumbered, books not a few, and courses of lectures. People who know beauty and love it are trying to teach it to those who do not, trying to introduce it where it is so painfully needed—in the home.

THE HOME

Why does it not originate there? Why did the people who cared most for beauty and art, the Greeks, care so little for the home? And why do the people who care most for the home—our Anglo-Saxons—care so little for beauty and art? And, in such art-knowledge and art-growth as we have, why is it least manifested at home? What is there in home-life, as we know it, which proves inimical to the development of true beauty? If there is some condition in home life which is inimical to art, is that condition essential and permanent, or may it be removed without loss to what is essential and permanent?

Here are questions serious and practical; practical because beauty is an element of highest use as well as joy. Our love of it lies deep, and rests on truest instinct; the child feels it passionately; the savage feels it, we all feel it, but few understand it; and whether we understand it or not we long for it in vain. We often make our churches beautiful, our libraries and museums, but our domestic efforts are not crowned with the same relative success.

The reasons for this innate lack of beauty in the home are not far to seek. The laws of applied beauty reach deep, spread wide, and are inexorable: Truth; first, last, and always—no falsehood, imitation, or pretence: Simplicity; no devious meandering, but the direct clear pur-

[144]

pose and result: Unity, Harmony, that unerring law of relation which keeps the past true to the whole—never too much here or there—all balanced and at rest: Restraint; no riotous excess, no rush from inadequacy to profusion.

If the student of art rightly apprehends these laws, his whole life is richer and sounder as well as his art. If the art he studies is one under definite laws of construction, he has to learn them, too; as in architecture, where the laws of mechanics operate with those of æsthetics, and there is no beauty if the mechanical laws are defied.

Architecture is the most prominent form of domestic art. Why is not domestic architecture as good as public architecture? If the home is a temple, why should not our hills be dotted with fair shrines worthy of worship?

We may talk as we will of " the domestic shrine," but the architect does not find the kitchen stove an inspiring altar. If it did inspire him, if he began to develop the idea of a kitchen—a temple to Hygeia and Epicurus, a great central altar for the libations and sacrifices, with all appropriate accessories for the contributory labour of the place—he could not make a pocket-edition of this temple, and stick it on to every house in forced connection with the other domestic necessities.

THE HOME

The eating-room then confronts him, a totally different *motif*. We do not wish to eat in the kitchen. We do not wish to see, smell, hear, or think of the kitchen while we eat. So the domestic architect is under the necessity of separating as far as possible these discordant purposes, while obliged still to confine them to the same walls and roof.

Then come the bedrooms. We do not wish to sleep in the kitchen—or in the dining-room. Nothing is further from our ideals than to confound the sheets with the tablecloths, the bed with the stove, the dressing table with the sink. So again the architect, whose kitchen-tendency was so rudely checked by the dining-room tendency, is brought up standing by the bedroom tendency, its demand for absolute detachment and remoteness, and the necessity for keeping its structural limits within those same walls and roof.

Then follows the reception-room tendency—we do not wish to receive our visitors in the kitchen—or the bedroom—or exclusively in the dining-room. So the parlour theme is developed as far as may be, connected with the dining-room, and disconnected as far as possible from all the other life-themes going on under that roof.

When we add to these the limits of space, especially in our cities, the limits of money, so almost universal, and the limits of personal taste, we may have clearly before us the reasons why domestic architecture does not thrill the soul with its beauty.

Whenever it does, to any extent, the reason is as clear. The feudal castle was beautiful because it had one predominant idea—defence; and was a stone monument to that idea. Here you could have truth, and did have it. Defence was imperative, absolute; every other need was subsidiary; a fine type of castle could give room for unity, simplicity, harmony, and restraint; and stirs us yet to delighted admiration. But it was not a comfortable dwelling-house.

A cottage is also capable of giving the sense of beauty; especially an old thatch-roofed cottage; mossy, mouldy, leaky, damp. The cottage is an undifferentiated home; it is primarily a kitchen—with a bedroom or two added—or included! Small primitive houses, like the white, square, flat-roofed dwellings of Algiers, group beautifully, or, taken singly, give a good bit of white against blue fire, behind green foliage.

But as a theme in itself, a thing to study and make pictures of the castle, the temple of war, is the most beautiful type of dwelling place—and the least inhabitable. In our really comfortable homes we have lost beauty, though we have gained in comfort. Would it be possible to have comfort and beauty too; beauty which would thrill and exalt us, delight and satisfy us, and which the art critic would dwell upon as he now does on temple, hall, and church?

Let us here take up the other domestic arts; surrendering architecture as apparently hopeless. We cannot expect our composers in wood and stone to take a number of absolutely contradictory themes and produce an effect of truth, unity, harmony, simplicity, and restraint; but may we not furnish and decorate our homes beautifully? Perhaps we might; but do we? What do we know, what do we care, for the elementary laws which make this thing beautiful, that thing ugly, and the same things vary as they are combined with others!

In the furnishing and decoration of a home we have room for more harmony than in the exterior, because each room may be treated separately according to its especial purpose, and we can accustom ourselves to the æsthetic jar of stepping from one to another, or even bring them all under some main scheme.

But here we are confronted by the enormous unrestricted weight of the limitation which is felt least by the architect—personal taste. We do not dictate much to our builders, most of us; but we do dictate as to the inside of the house and all that is in it. The dominating influence in home decoration is of course the woman. She is the final arbiter of the textures, colours, proportions, sizes, shapes, and relations of human production. How does she effect our output? What is her influence upon art—the applied art that is found, or should be found, in everything we make and use?

We may buy, if we can afford it, specimens of art, pictorial or sculptural art, or any other, and place them in our houses; but the mere accumulation of beautiful objects is not decoration; often quite the contrary. There are many beautiful vases in the shop where you bought yours; there is but one in the Japanese room—and there is beauty.

The magpie instinct of the collector has no part in a genuine sense of beauty. An ostentatious exhibit of one's valuable possessions does not show the sense of beauty. A beautiful chamber is neither show-room nor museum. That personal " taste " in itself is no guide to beauty needs but little proof. The " taste " of the Flathead Indian, of the tattooed Islander, of all the grades of physical deformity which mankind has admired, is sufficient to show that a personal preference is no ground for judgment in beauty.

Beauty has laws, and an appreciation of them is not possessed equally by all. The more primitive and ignorant a race, or class, the less it knows of true beauty.

The Indian basket-makers wove beautiful things, but they did not know it; give them the cheap and ugly productions of our greedy " market " and they like them better. They may unconsciously produce beauty, but they do not consciously select it.

Our women are far removed from the primitive simplicity that produces unconscious beauty; and they are also far removed from that broad culture and wide view of life which can intellectually grasp it. They have neither the natural instinct nor the acquired knowledge of beauty; but they do have, in million-fold accumulation, a " personal taste." The life of the woman in the home is absolutely confined to personal details. Her field of study and of work is not calculated to develop large judgment, but is calculated to develop intense feeling; and feeling on a comparatively low plane. She is forced continually to contemplate and minister to the last details of the physical wants of humanity in ceaseless daily repetition. Whatever tendency to develop artistic feeling and judgment she might have in one line of her work, is ruthlessly contradicted by the next, and the next; and her range of expression in each line is too small to allow of any satisfying growth.

DOMESTIC ART

The very rich woman who can purchase others' things and others' judgment, or the exceptional woman who does work and study in some one line, may show development in the sense of beauty; but it is not produced at home. The love of it is there, the desire for it, most cruelly aborted; and the result of that starved beauty-sense is what we see in our familiar rooms.

Being familiar, we bear with our surroundings; perhaps even love them; when we go into each other's homes we do not think their things to be beautiful; we think ours are because we are used to them; we have no appreciation of an object in its relation to the rest, or its lack of relation.

The bottled discord of the woman's daily occupations is quite sufficient to account for the explosions of discord on her walls and floors. She continually has to do utterly inharmonious things, she lives in incessant effort to perform all at once and in the same place the most irreconcilable processes.

She has to adjust, disadjust, and readjust her mental focus a thousand times a day; not only to things, but to actions; not only to actions, but to persons; and so, to live at all, she must develop a kind of mind that does *not object to discord.* Unity, harmony, simplicity, truth, restraint—these are not applicable in a patchwork life, however hallowed by high devotion and tender love. This is why domestic art is so low—so indistinguishable.

When our great Centennial Exhibition was given us, a wave of beauty spread into thousands of homes, but it did not originate there. The White City by the lake was an inspiration to myriad lives, and wrought a lovely change in her architecture and many other arts; but the Black City by the Lake is there yet, waiting for another extra-domestic uplifting.

The currents of home-life are so many, so diverse, so contradictory, that they are only maintained by using the woman as a sort of universal solvent; and this position of holding many diverse elements in solution is not compatible with the orderly crystallisation of any of them, or with much peace of mind to the unhappy solvent.

The most conspicuous field for the display of the beauty sense—or the lack of it—in our home life, is in textile fabrics and their application to the body. The House is the foundation of textile art. People who live out of doors wear hides, if they wear anything. In the shelter and peace of the house, developed by ever-widening commerce, grew these wonderful textile arts, the evolution of a new plane for beauty. We find in nature nothing approaching it, save in the limited and passing form of spreading leaf and petal. To make a continuous substance soft as flowers, warm as furs, brilliant as the sunset—this was a great step in art.

Woven beauty is a home product, and in the house we are most free to use and admire it. The " street dress," even the most unsophisticated, is under some restrictions; but the house dress may be anything we please. There is nothing in the mechanical limitations of house life to pervert or check this form of loveliness. We are free to make and to use the most exquisite materials, to wear the most pleasing of textures and shapes.

Why, then, do we find in this line of development such hideously inartistic things? Because the discords of domestic industries and functions prevent a sense of harmony even here. Because the woman, confined to a primitive, a savage plane of occupation, continues to manifest an equally savage plane of æsthetic taste.

One of the most marked features of early savage decoration is in its distortion and mutilation of the body to meet arbitrary standards of supposed beauty. An idea of beauty, true or false, is apprehended, its line of special evolution rapidly followed, and there is no knowledge of physiology or grasp of larger harmonies of bodily grace to check the ensuing mutilation.

The Zulus decorate their cattle by cutting the dewlap

into fringe, and splitting and twisting the growing horns into fantastic shapes. Some savage women tie the gastrocnemius muscle tightly above and below, till the " calf of the leg " looks like a Dutch cheese on a broomstick. Some tie strings about the breasts till they dangle half detached; some file the teeth or pluck out the eyebrows.

In the home, among women, still appear these manifestations of a crude beauty-sense, unchecked by larger knowledge. Our best existent examples are in the Chinese foot-binding custom, and ours of waist-binding. The initial idea of the corset is in a way artistic. We perceive that the feminine form has certain curves and proportions, tending thus and so; and following the tendency we proceed to exaggerate those curves and proportions and fix them arbitrarily. This is the same law by which we conventionalise a flower for decorative purposes, turning the lily of the field into the *fleur-de-lis* of the tapestry. The Egyptians did it, to an extreme degree, in their pictorial art, reducing the human body to certain fixed proportions and attitudes.

The application of these principles to living bodies is peculiar to the savage, and its persistence among our women is perhaps the strongest proof of the primitive nature of the home. As women enter the larger life of the world these limitations are easily outgrown; the working-woman cannot make a conventionalised ornament of her body, and the business woman does not care to; the really educated woman knows better, and the woman artist would be bitterly ashamed of such an offence against nature; only the home-bound woman peacefully maintains it.

To the scientific student, man or woman, the sturdy reappearance of this very early custom is intensely interesting; he sees in the "newest fashion" of holding and binding the body a peculiar survival of the very oldest fashion in personal decoration known to us. The latest corset advertisement ranks ethnologically with the earliest Egyptian hieroglyph, the Aztec inscriptions, and races far behind them.

The woman's love of beauty finds its freest expression along lines of personal decorations, and there, as in the decoration of the house, we see the same crippling influence.

She loves beautiful textures, velvet, satin, and silk, soft muslin and sheer lawn; she loves the delicate fantasy of lace, the alluring richness of fur; she loves the colour and sparkle of gems, the splendour of burnished metal, and, in her savage crudity of taste, she slaps together any and every combination of these things and wears them happily.

THE HOME

A typical extreme of this ingenuous lack of artistic principles is the recent, and still present, enormity of trimming lace with fur. This combines the acme of all highly wrought refinement of texture and exquisite delicacy of design, a fabric that suggests the subtleties of artistic expression with a gossamer tenuity of grace; this, and dressed hide with the hair still on, the very first cover for man's nakedness, the symbol of savage luxury and grandeur, of raw barbaric wealth, which suggests warmth, ample satisfying warmth and crude splendour in its thick profusion! We cut up the warmth and amplitude into threads and scraps which can only suggest the gleanings of a tan-yard rag-picker, and use these shabby fragments to *trim lace!* Trim what is in itself the sublimated essence of trimming, with the leavings of the earliest of raw materials! Only the soul which spends its life in a group of chambers connected merely by mechanical force; in a group of industries connected merely by iron tradition, could bear a combination like that— to say nothing of enjoying it. Domestic art is almost a contradiction in terms.

The development of art, like the development of industry, requires the specialisation, the life-long devotion, impossible to the arbitrary combinations of home life. Where you find great beauty you find a great civic sense, most clearly in that high-water mark of human progress in this direction, ancient Greece. Within the limits of their cities, the Greeks were more fully " civilised " than any people before or since. They thought, felt, and acted in this large social contact; and so developed a sufficient breadth of view, a wide, sweet sanity of mind, which allowed of this free growth of the art-sense. Great art is always public, and appears only in periods of high social development. The one great art of the dark ages —religious architecture—flourished in that universal atmosphere of " Christendom," the one social plane on which all met.

The Greeks were unified in many ways; and their highly socialised minds gave room for a more general development of art, as well as many other social faculties.

Household decoration was not conspicuous, nor elaborate attire; and while their women were necessarily beautiful as the daughters of such men, it was the men whose beauty was most admired and immortalised. The women stayed at home, as now, but the home did not absorb men, too, as it does now. When art caters to private tastes, to domestic tastes, to the wholly private and domestic tastes of women, art goes down.

The Home was the birthplace of Art, as of so many other human faculties, but is no sufficing area for it. So long as the lives of our woman are spent at home, their tastes limited by it, their abilities, ambitions, and desires limited by it, so long will the domestic influence lower art.

" So much the worse for art!" will stoutly cry the defenders of the home; and they would be right if we could have but one. We can have both.

A larger womanhood, a civilised womanhood, specialised, broad-minded, working and caring for the public good *as well as the private*, will give us not only better homes, but homes more beautiful. The child will be cradled in an atmosphere of harmonious loveliness, and its influence will be felt in all life. This is no trifle of an artificially cultivated æsthetic taste; it is one of nature's deepest laws. " Art " may vary and suffer in different stages of our growth, but the laws of beauty remain the same; and a race reared under those laws will be the nobler.

These more developed women will outgrow the magpie taste that hoards all manner of gay baubles; the monkey-taste that imitates whatever it sees; the savage taste that distorts the human body; they will recognise in that body one infinitely noble expression of beauty, and refuse to dishonour it with ugliness.

They will learn to care for proportion as well as plumpness, for health as well as complexion, for strength

DOMESTIC ART

and activity as essentials to living loveliness, and to see that no dress can be beautiful which in any way contradicts the body it should but serve and glorify. We do not know, because we have not seen, the difference to our lives which will be made by this large sense of beauty in the woman—in the home; but we may be assured that, while she stays continually there, we shall have but our present stage of domestic art.

IX

DOMESTIC ETHICS

THE relation of the home to ethics is so vital, so intimate, so extensive, as to call for the utmost care and patience in its study.

The " domestic virtues " are well known to us, and well loved. We have a general conviction that all our virtues as well as charity begin at home; that the ethical progress of man is a steady stream flowing out of the home, and as far as we compare one virtue with another, we assume the domestic virtues to be the best.

In half the race we ask nothing but the domestic virtues; in the other half we look for something further; but consider such civic and social virtues as appear to be offshoots of the domestic. We call the home " the cradle of all the virtues," and never imagine for a moment that it can cradle anything else—in the line of ethics.

Now let us make a careful examination of this field; first establishing a standard of human conduct and character, and then studying the relation of the home to that standard. The same consideration referred to in previous chapters is here most urgently pressed upon the reader: that all the qualities found in the home do not necessarily originate there. As a race rises and improves, its improvement appears in the home, as elsewhere. But that improvement is in itself due to varying conditions. The diffusion of intelligence following the discovery of the art of printing lifted the general average mind, and so lifted the home as well as other departments of life. But that increase of intelligence did not originate in home life, and is in no way due to its influence.

The sense of human liberty which spread rapidly among us in the early years of the settlement of this country, following, as it did, the splendid dash for religious liberty which brought so many of our ancestors here, has borne fruit in our home life. We have more freedom in the family relation than is found in older forms of government, but this larger freedom did not originate in the home and is in no way to be accredited to it.

Home-life, as such, does in itself tend to produce certain ethical qualities; qualities not produced, or not in any such degree, by other fields of life. Constant association with helpless infancy develops a generous care and kindness—that is, it does so when the helpless infants are one's own. The managers of foundling and orphan asylums do not seem always to be so affected. Constant association with the inevitable errors and mistakes of childhood develops patience and sympathy, or tends to do so. There are qualities brought out in home life which extend their influence into the life of the world. The young man or woman who has had good home influence shows that advantage all through life. But there are also qualities brought out in the world's life apart from the home; and the man or woman affected by these shows them in the home life. We find in our homes the gathered flowers of civilisation, of Christianity, of progress in general; and unconsciously accredit the homes with the production of these beautiful results—quite erroneously.

The influence of religion, as we all know when we stop to think of it, has done much more for us than the influence of the home. The Canaanites had homes—yet gave their children to Moloch. The demand of the idol had more power than the appeal of the child. The Hindoos have homes, yet give their babies to the water, their widows to the fire.

Besides religion there are many other influences which affect human character and conduct; the influences of our government, our education, our business. We are seeking here to point out precisely what ethical qualities are

[162]

developed by home life, good or bad; and to show further that the present condition of the home is not final, nor vitally essential. We may so change the conditions of home life as to retain all that modifies character for good, and to discard all that modifies it for evil.

The home as a permanent institution in society, if rightly placed and understood, works for good. The home in its non-essential conditions, if wrongly placed in our scheme of thought, if misunderstood, if out of proportion and loaded with anachronisms, works evil. In the complex group of qualities which make up the human character to-day, for good and ill, many influences are traceable; and we wish here to disentangle from among them some lines of influence, and show what place is held by the home in making us what we are and what we wish to be.

What is the preferred type of excellence in humanity according to our social instincts and to the measure of history? We began as savages, and the savage standard of ethics is easily grasped; we have progressed a long way beyond that savage standard; but ours is still well within the reach of common understanding. Without seeking for careful sequence let us enumerate our principal human virtues:

THE HOME

Love; with derivatives of kindness, sympathy, courtesy, etc. Truth; with honesty, accuracy, etc. Courage; connects with strength and wisdom. Justice; with a right humility. Self-control; with endurance, patience, and again with courtesy; also with temperance and chastity. Honour; a high, inflexible standard of various virtues.

These are arbitrary general types, but do fairly enough for this study. A human being possessed of these in high degree we should call " good." They all combine well with one another, and have many derivatives, some of which are above noted. Their common opposites are as easily given:

Hate; unkindness, coldness, rudeness. Falsehood; lying, dishonesty, inaccuracy. Cowardice; connects with weakness and ignorance. Injustice; this allows pride—rests on ignorance. Self-indulgence; followed by intemperance, unchastity, impatience, and other vices. Dishonour; meaning a low standard of virtues in general.

Man the savage had of these courage, in some lines; endurance and patience, in some lines; civilised man surpasses him in these, and has developed all the others. What are the conditions which have brought forth this degree of virtue in us, and how does the home rank among those conditions?

DOMESTIC ETHICS

Let us first do it full justice. Mother-love is the foundation and permanent force of home life; and, mother-love is, indeed, the parent of all the love we know. Altruism was born of babyhood. The continued existence of the child—of a succession of children; the permanent presence of helplessness and its irresistible demands for care; this forced us into a widening of the sympathies, a deepening of sensitiveness to others' needs; this laid the foundations of human love. In this sense, the home is the cradle of one of our very greatest virtues. Love began with the mother; but it should not stop with her. "Mother-love" is precisely limited to its own children.

Few, indeed, are the mothers who love other women's children. As "mother" is a synonym for all kindness, so "stepmother" is a synonym for all unkindness. Folklore and fairy-tale indicate old fact. Infant helplessness and orphan need are not only what appeals to the mother—it is most the blood-tie, the physical relation.

Civilisation and Christianity teach us to care for "the child," motherhood stops at "my child."

Still, in the home we do find the nursery of all the lines of family affection, parental, filial, fraternal, and these are good. Hearts able to love ten could more easily take in twenty; the love of one's own parents spread to our present care for the aged; the power of loving grew, and, as soon as it overstepped the limits of the home, it grew more rapidly. We have learned to love our neighbours—if not as ourselves, at least, better than strangers. We have learned to love our fellow-citizens, fellow-craftsmen, fellow-countrymen. To-day the first thrills of international good-will are stealing across the world—and we are extending our sympathy even to the animals.

All this beautiful growth of love began at home; but the influence of the home, as it now exists upon the growth, is not so wholly gratifying. The love that we call human, the love of one another, the love Christ teaches us, is extra-domestic. We are not told, " Inasmuch as you have done it to your own families you have done it unto me." We are not exhorted to an ever-increasing intensity of devotion to our own blood-relations.

Both the teaching of our religion and the tendency of social progress call for a larger love, and the home, in its position of arrested development, primitive industry, and crippled womanhood, tends rather to check that growth than to help it. The man's love for his family finds expression in his labour for other people— he serves society, and society provides for him and his dear ones; so good will spreads and knits; comradeship and fellow-feeling appear, friendship brings its pure height of affection; this is the natural line of development in the great social virtue, love.

But the woman, still expressing her love for her family in direct personal service, misses all that. The primitive father, to feed the child, went forth himself and killed some rabbit—and the primitive mother cooked it: love, in grade A. The modern father, to feed his child, takes his thousandth part in some complex industry, and receives his thousand-fold share of the complex products of others' industry, and so provides for the child far more richly than could the savage: love, in grade Z. But the modern mother—if we can call her so by courtesy—to feed her child still does nothing but cook for it, still loves in grade A; and the effect of that persistence of grade A is to retard the development of grade Z. Mother-love is the fountain of all our human affection; but mother-love, *as limited by the home*, does not have the range and efficacy proper to our time. The home, as at present maintained, checks the growth of love.

As to Truth. This is a distinctly modern virtue. It comes in slowly, following power and freedom. The weak lie, a small beast hides; the lion does not hide.

[167]

The slave lies—and the courtier; the king does not lie—he does not need to.

The most truthful nations are the most powerful. The most truthful class is the most powerful. The more truthful sex is the more powerful. Weakness, helplessness, ignorance, dependence, these breed falsehood and evasion; and, in child, servant, and woman, the denizens of the home, we have to combat these tendencies. The standard of sincerity of the father may be taught the son; but the home is not the originator of that standard. In this, as in other virtues, gain made in quite other fields of growth is necessarily transmitted to the home; but fair analysis must discriminate between the effect of religion, of education, of new social demands, and the effect of the home as such.

Courage comes along two main lines—by exposure to danger, and by increase of strength. The home, in its very nature, is intended to shield from danger; it is in origin a hiding place, a shelter for the defenceless. Staying in it is in no way conducive to the growth of courage. Constant shelter, protection, and defence may breed gratitude—must breed cowardice. We expect timidity of " women and children "—the housemates. Yet courage is by no means a sex attribute. Every species of animal that shows courage shows it equally in male and female—or even more in mother than in father. "It is better to meet a she-bear robbed of her whelps than a fool in his folly." This dominant terror—the fool—is contrasted with the female bear—not the male. Belligerence, mere combativeness, is a masculine attribute; but courage is not.

The cowardice of women is a distinctly home product. It is born of weakness and ignorance; a weakness and an ignorance by no means essential feminine attributes, but strictly domestic attributes. Keep a man from birth wrapped in much cloth, shut away from sky and sun, wind and rain, continually exhausting his nervous energy by incessant activity in monotonous little things, and never developing his muscular strength and skill by suitable exercise of a large and varied nature, and he would be weak. Savage women are not weak. Peasant women are not weak. Fishwives are not weak. The home-bound woman is weak, as would be a home-bound man. Also, she is ignorant. Not, at least not nowadays, ignorant necessarily of books, but ignorant of general life.

It is this ignorance and this weakness which makes women cowards; cowards frank and unashamed; cowards accustomed to be petted and praised, to be called "true woman" because they scream at that arch-terror

[169]

of the home—a mouse. This home-bred cowardice, so admired in women, is of necessity transmitted to their sons as well as daughters. It is laughed out of them and knocked out of them, but it is born into them, relentlessly, with every generation. As black mothers must alter the complexion of a race, so must coward mothers alter its character. Apart from fighting—where the natural combative sex-tendency often counts as courage—our men are not as brave as they would be if their mothers were braver. We need courage to-day as much as we ever needed it in our lives. Courage to think and speak the truth; courage to face convention and prejudice, ridicule and opposition. We need courage in men and women equally, to face the problems of the times; and we do not get that courage from the home.

The sense of Justice is one of the highest human attributes; one of the latest in appearance, one of the rarest and most precious. We love and honour justice; we seek in some main lines of life to enforce it, after a fashion; but many of our arrangements are still so palpably unjust that one would think the virtue was but dreamed of, as yet unborn. Justice follows equality and freedom. To apprehend it at all the mind must first perceive the equal, and then resent the unequal. We must get a sense of level, of balance, and then we notice a deflection. As a matter of social evolution our system of legal justice springs from the primitive market place, the disputes of equals, the calling in of a third party to adjudicate. The disputants know instinctively that an outsider can see the difficulty better than an insider. Slowly the arbiter was given more power, more scope; out of much experience came the crystallisation of law. "Justice!" was the cry of the lowest before the highest; and the greatest kings were honoured most for this great virtue.

The field for justice has widened as the state widened; it has reached out to all classes; its high exercise distinguishes the foremost nations of our times. Yet even in the teeth of the law-courts injustice is still common; in everyday life it is most patent.

We have made great progress in the sense of justice and fair play; yet we are still greatly lacking in it. What is the contribution of domestic ethics to this mighty virtue? In the home is neither freedom nor equality. There is ownership throughout; the dominant father, the more or less subservient mother, the utterly dependent child; and sometimes that still lower grade— the servant. Love is possible, love deep and reciprocal; loyalty is possible; gratitude is possible; kindness, to ruinous favouritism, is possible; unkindness, to all con-

[171]

spiracy, hate, and rebellion is possible; justice is not possible.

Justice was born outside the home and a long way from it; and it has never even been adopted there.

Justice is wholly social in its nature—extra-domestic —even anti-domestic. Just men may seek to do justly in their homes, but it is hard work. Intense, personal feeling, close ties of blood, are inimical to the exercise of justice. Do we expect the judge upon the bench to do justice, dispassionate, unswerving, on his own child—his own wife—in the dock? If he does, we hail him as more than mortal. Do we expect a common man—not a judge with all the training and experience of his place, but a plain man—to do justice to his own wife and his own child in the constant intimacy of the home? Do we expect the mother to do justice to the child when the child is the offender and the mother the offended? Where plaintiff, judge, and executioner are lodged in one person; where there is no third party—no spectators even— only absolute irresponsible power, why should we—how could we—expect justice! We don't. We do not even think of it. No child cries for " Justice! " to the deaf walls of the home—he never heard of it.

He gets love—endless love and indulgence. He gets anger and punishment with no court of appeal.

He gets care—neglect—discourtesy—affection—indifference—cruelty—and sometimes wise and lovely training—but none of these are justice. The home, as such, in no way promotes justice; but, in its disproportionate and unbalanced position to-day, palpably perverts and prevents it.

Allied to justice, following upon large equality and recognition of others, comes that true estimate of one's self and one's own powers which is an unnamed virtue. "Humility" is not it—to undervalue and depreciate one's self may be the opposite of pride, but it is not a virtue. A just estimate is not humility. But call it humility for convenience' sake; and see how ill it flourishes at home. In that circumscribed horizon small things look large. There is no general measuring point, no healthy standard of comparison.

The passionate love of the wife, the mother, and equally of the husband, the father, makes all geese swans. The parents idealise their children; and the children, even more restricted by the home atmosphere—*for they know no other*—idealise the parents. This is sometimes to their advantage—often the other way. Constant study of near objects, with no distant horizon to rest and change the focus, makes us short-sighted; and, as we all know, the smallest object is large if you hold it near enough. Constant association with one's nearest and dearest necessarily tends to a disproportionate estimate of their values.

There is no perspective—cannot be—in these close quarters. The infant prodigy of talent, praised and petted, brings his production into the cold light of the market, under the myriad facets of the public eye, to the measurement of professional standards—and no most swift return to the home atmosphere can counterbalance the effect of that judgment day. A just estimate of one's self and one's work can only be attained by the widest and most impersonal comparison. The home estimate is essentially personal, essentially narrow. It sometimes errs in underrating a world-talent; but nine times out of ten it errs the other way—overrating a home-talent. Humility, in the sense of an honest and accurate estimate of one's self, is not a home-made product. A morbid modesty or an unfounded pride often is. The intense self-consciousness, the prominent and sensitive personality developed by home life, we are all familiar with in women.

The woman who has always been in close personal relation with someone,—daughter, sister, wife, mother,—and so loved, valued, held close, feels herself neglected and chilly when she comes into business relations. She feels personal neglect in the broad indifference of office or shop; and instantly seeks to establish personal relations with all about her. As a business woman she outgrows it in time. It is not a sex-quality, it is a home-quality; found in a boy brought up entirely at home as well as in a girl. It tends to a disproportionate estimate of self; it is a primitive quality, common to children and savages; it is not conducive to justice and true social adjustment.

Closely allied to this branch of character is the power of self-control. As an initial human virtue none lies deeper than this; and here the home has credit for much help in developing some of the earlier stages of this great faculty. Primitive man brought to his dawning human relation a long-descended, highly-developed Ego. He had been an individual animal " always and always," he had now to begin to be a social animal, a collective animal, to develop the social instincts and the social conduct in which lay further progress.

The training of the child shows us in little what history shows us in the large. What the well-bred child has to learn to make him a pleasing member of the family is self-control. To restrain and adjust one's self to one's society—that is the line of courtesy—the line of Christianity—the line of social evolution. The home life does indeed teach the beginning of self-control; but no more. As compared with the world, it represents unbridled license. " In company " one must wear so and so, talk so and so, do so and so, look so and so. To " feel at home " means relaxation of all this.

This is as it should be. The home is the place for personal relief and rest from the higher plane of social contact. But social contact is needed to develop social qualities, constant staying at home does not do it.

The man, accustomed to meet all sorts of people in many ways, has a far larger and easier adjustment. The woman, used only to the close contact of a few people in a few relations, as child, parent, servant, tradesman; or to the set code of " company manners," has no such healthy human plane of contact.

" I never was so treated in my life! " she complains— and she never was—at home. This limits the range of life, cuts off the widest channels of growth, overdevelops the few deep ones; and does not develop self-control. The dressing-gown-and-slippers home attitude is temporarily changed for that of " shopping," or " visiting," but the childish sensitiveness, the disproportionate personality, remain dominant.

A too continuous home atmosphere checks in the woman the valuable social faculties. It checks it in the man more insidiously, through his position of easy mastery over these dependents, wife, children, servants; and through the constant catering of the whole *ménage* to his special tastes. If each man had a private tailor shop in his back yard he would be far more whimsical and exacting in his personal taste in clothes. Every natural tendency to self-indulgence is steadily increased by the life service of an entire wife. This having one whole woman devoted to one's direct personal service is about as far from the cultivation of self-control as any process that could be devised.

The man loves the woman and serves her—but he serves her *through his service of the world*—and she serves him direct. He can fuss and dictate as to details, he can develop all manner of notions as to bacon, or toast, or griddle cakes; the whole cuisine is his, he supports it, it is meant to please him, and under its encompassing temptation he increases in girth and weight; but not in self-control. He may be a wise, temperate, judicious man, but the home, with its disproportionate attention to personal desires, does not make him so.

No clearer instance could be given of the effect of domestic ethics. In this one field may be shown the beneficent effects of the early home upon early man, the continued beneficent effects of what is essential in the home upon modern man; and the most evil effects of the domestic rudiments upon modern man. The differing ages and sexes held together by love, yet respecting one another's privacy, demand of one another precisely this power of self-control. Children together, with no adults, become boisterous and unruly; adults together, with no children, become out of sympathy with childhood; the sexes, separated, tend to injurious excesses; but the true home life checks excess, develops what is lacking, harmonises all.

What does the morbid, disproportioned, overgrown home life do? It tends to develop a domineering selfishness in man and a degrading abnegation in woman— or sometimes reverses this effect. The smooth, unconscious, all-absorbing greed which the unnaturally developed home of to-day produces in some women, is as evil a thing as life shows. Here is a human creature who has all her life been loved and cared for, sheltered, protected, defended; everything provided for her and nothing demanded of her except the exercise of her natural feminine functions, and some proficiency in the playground regulations of " society."

The degree of sublimated selfishness thus produced by home life is quite beyond the selfishness we so deplore in

[178]

men. A man may be—often is—deplorably selfish in his home life; but he does not expect all the world to treat him with the same indulgence. He has to give as well as take in the broad, healthy, growing life of the world.

The woman has her home-life to make her selfish, and has no world life to offset it. Men are polite to her on account of her sex—not on account of any power, any achievement, any distinctive human value, but simply because she is a woman. Her guests are necessarily polite to her. Her hosts are necessarily polite to her, and so are her fellow-guests. Her servants are necessarily polite to her. Her children also; if they are not she feels herself abused, denied a right.

The home and its social tributaries steadily work to develop a limitless personal selfishness in which the healthy power of self-control is all unknown. One way or the other swings the pendulum; here the woman pours out her life in devotion to her husband and children; in which case she is developing selfishness in them with as much speed and efficacy as if she were their worst enemy; and here again the woman sits, plump and fair, in her padded cage, bedizening its walls with every decoration; covering her own body with costly and beautiful things; feeding herself, her family, her guests; running from

[179]

meal to meal as if eating were really the main business of a human being. This is the extreme.

Our primitive scheme requires that the entire time of the woman-who-does-her-own-work shall be spent in ministering to the physical needs of her family; and in the small minority who have other women to do it for them, that she shall still have this ministry her main care—and shall have no others. It is this inordinate demand for the life and time of a whole woman to keep half a dozen people fed, cleaned, and waited on, which keeps up in us a degree of self-indulgence we should, by every step of social development, have long since outgrown.

The personal preparation of food by a loving wife and mother does not ensure right nourishment—that we have shown at length; but it does ensure that every human soul thus provided for shall give far too much thought to what it eats and drinks and wherewithal it shall be clothed. The yielding up of a woman's life to the service of these physical needs of mankind does not develop self-control, nor its noble line of ensuing virtues—temperance, chastity, courtesy, patience, endurance.

See the child growing up under this disproportionate attention; fussy, critical, capricious, always thinking

[180]

of what he wants and how he wants it. The more his mother waits on him, the more she has to do so; he knows no better than to help himself to the offered life. See the husband, criticising the coffee and the steak; or so enjoying and praising them that the happy wife eagerly spends more hours in preparing more dishes that John will like. It is a pleasant, roseate atmosphere. All are happy in it. Why is it not good? Because it is a hotbed of self-indulgence. Because it constantly maintains a degree of personal devotion to one's appetites which would disappear under a system of living suited to our age.

Self-control is developed by true home life; by true family love. Family, love, unmodified by social relation, gives also the family feud; the unconscionably narrow pride of the clansman; the home life of the first century, arbitrarily maintained in the twentieth, gives us its constant contribution of first-century ethics.

As to honour—that delicate, deep-rooted, instinctive ethical sense; applied so rigidly to this, so little to that; showing so variously; " business honour," " military honour," " professional honour," " the honour of a gentleman "—what is the standard of honour in the home?

The only " honour " asked of the woman is chastity;

quite a special sex-distinction, not as yet demanded in any great degree of the man.

If the home develops chastity, it seems to discriminate sharply in its preferred exponent. But apart from that virtue, what sense of honour do we find in the home-bound woman? Is it to keep her word inflexibly? A woman's privilege is to change her mind. Is it to spare the weaker? Would that some dream of this high grace could stand between the angry woman and the defenceless child. Is it to respect privacy, to scorn eavesdropping, to regard the letter of another person as inviolate?

The standard of honour in the home is not that of " an officer and a gentleman." The things a decent and well-educated woman will sometimes do to her own children, do cheerfully and unblushingly, are flatly dishonourable; but she does not even know it. And the things she does outside the home, with only her home-bred sense of honour to guide her, are equally significant. To slip in front of others who are standing in line; to make engagements and break them; to even engage rooms and board, and then change her plans without letting the other party know; thus entailing absolute money loss to a perfectly innocent person, without a qualm; this is frequently done by women with a high standard of chastity; but no other sense of honour whatever.

The home is the cradle of all the virtues, but we are in a stage of social development where we need virtues beyond the cradle size. The virtues begun at home need to come out and grow in the world as men need to do—and as woman need to do, but do not know it. The ethics of the home are good in degree. The ethics of human life are far larger and more complex.

Our moral growth is to-day limited most seriously by the persistent maintenance in half the world of a primitive standard of domestic ethics.

X

DOMESTIC ENTERTAINMENT

LONG is the way from the primal home, with its
simple child-*motif*, to the large and expensive
house of entertainment we call home to-day.
The innocent "guest-chamber" early added to the family
accommodations has spread its area and widened its demands, till we find the ultra-type of millionaire mansion
devoting its whole space, practically, to the occupation
of guests—for even the private rooms are keyed up to a
comparison with those frankly built and furnished for
strangers. The kitchen, the dining-room, the pantry,
the table-furniture of all sorts, are arranged in style and
amplitude to meet the needs of guests. The sitting-room
becomes a " parlour," the parlour a " drawing-room "
with " reception-room " addition; and then comes the
still more removed " ballroom "—a remarkable apartment truly, to form part of a home. Some even go so
far as to add a theatre—that most essentially public of
chambers—in this culminating transformation of a home
to a house of entertainment.

From what once normal base sprang this abnormal

growth? How did this place of love and intimacy, the outward form of our most tender and private relations, so change and swell to a place of artificial politeness and most superficial contact? The point of departure is not hard to find; it lies in that still visible period when hospitality was one of our chief virtues.

Of all the evolving series of human virtues none is more easily studied in its visible relation to condition and its rapid alterations than hospitality. Moreover, though considered a virtue, it is not so intermingled with our deepest religious sanction as to be painful to discuss; we respect, but do not worship it.

Hospitality is a quality of human life, a virtue which appears after a certain capacity for altruism is developed; not a very high degree, for we find a rigid code of hospitality among many savage tribes; and which obtains in exact proportion to the distance, difficulty, and danger of travelling.

We still find its best type among the Bedouin Arabs and the Scotch Highlanders; we find it in our own land more in the country than the city, more in the thinly settled and poorly roaded south than in the more thickly settled and better roaded north; and most of all on the western frontier, where mountain and desert lie between ranch and ranch.

THE HOME

To call out the most lively sense of hospitality the traveller must be weary (that means a long, hard road), and " distressed "—open to injury, if not hospitably received. To have a fresh, clean, rosy traveller drop in after half an hour's pleasant stroll does not touch the springs of hospitality. The genuine figure to call out this virtue is the stranger, the wanderer, the pilgrim.

Hospitality will not stand constant use. The steady visitor must be a friend; and friendship is quite a different thing from hospitality. That finds its typical instance in the old Scotch chief sheltering the hunted fugitive; and defending him against his pursuers even when told that his guest was the murderer of his son. As guest he was held sacred; he had claimed the rights of hospitality and he received them. Had he returned to make the same demand every few days, even without renewing his initial offence, it is doubtful if hospitality would have held out.

A somewhat thin, infrequent virtue is hospitality at its heights, requiring intervals of relaxation. " Withdraw thy foot from thy neighbour's house, lest he weary of thee and hate thee," says the proverb of the very people where the laws of hospitality were sacred; and " the stranger within thy gates " came under the regular provision of household law.

DOMESTIC ENTERTAINMENT

Hospitality became a sort of standing custom under feudalism, as part of the parental care of the Lord of the Land; and thus acquired its elements of pride and ostentation. Each nobleman owned all the land about him; the traveller had to claim shelter of him either directly or through his dependents, and the castle was the only place big enough for entertainment. The nobleman saw to it that no other person on his domain should be able to offer much hospitality. So the Castle or the Abbey had it all.

A little of this spirit gave character to the partly danger-based southern hospitality. It was necessary to the occasional stranger on the original and legitimate grounds; it became a steady custom to the modern Lord of the Manor, none of whose subsidiary fellow-citizens had the wherewithal to feed and shelter guests. But hospitality, even in that form, is not what issues cards and lays red carpet under awnings from door to curb.

Here no free-handed cordial greeting keeps the visitor to dinner—the dinner where the plates are named and numbered and the caterer ready with due complement of each expensive dish. Hospitality must blush and apologise—" I'm sorry, but you must excuse me, I have to dress for dinner!" and " Why, of course! I forgot it was so late!—dear me! the Jenkinses will have come before me if I don't hurry home!" On what ground, then, is that dinner given—why are the Jenkinses asked that night? If not the once sacred spirit of hospitality, is it the still sacred spirit of friendship?

Are the people we so expensively and elaborately entertain—and who so carefully retaliate, card for card, *plat* for *plat* and dollar for dollar—are these the people whom we love? Among our many guests is an occasional friend. The occasional friend we entreat to come and see us *when we are not entertaining!*

Friendships are the fruit of true personal expression, the drawing together that follows recognition, the manifest kinships of the outspoken soul. In friendship we discriminate, we particularise, we enjoy the touch and interchange of like characteristics, the gentle stimulus of a degree of unlikeness. Friendship comes naturally, spontaneously, along lines of true expression in work, of a casual propinquity that gives rein to the unforced thought. More friendships are formed in the prolonged association of school-life or business life, in the intimacy of a journey together or a summer's camping, than ever grew in a lonely lifetime of crowded receptions. Friendship may coexist with entertainment, may even thrive in spite of it, but is neither cause nor result of that strange process.

DOMESTIC ENTERTAINMENT

What, then, is " entertainment," to which the home is sacrificed so utterly—which is no part of fatherhood, motherhood, or childhood, of hospitality or friendship?

On what line of social evolution may we trace the growth of this amazing phenomenon; this constant gathering together of many people to eat when they are not hungry, dance when they are not merry, talk when they have nothing to say, and sit about so bored by their absurd position that the hostess must needs hire all manner of paid performers wherewith to " entertain " them?

Here is the explanation: humanity is a relation. It is not merely a number of human beings, like a number of grains of sand. The human being, to be really human, must be associated in various forms; grouped together in the interchange of function. The family relation, as we have seen, does not in itself constitute humanity; human relations are larger.

Man, as a separate being, the personal man, must have his private house to be separate in. Man, as a collective being, the social man, must have his public house to be together in. This does not mean a drinking place, but any form of building which shelters our common social functions. A church is a public house—in it we meet together as human beings; as individuals, not as families; to perform the common social function of wor-

[189]

ship. All religions have this collective nature—people come together as human beings, under a common impulse.

The home is a private house. That belongs to us separately for the fulfilment of purely personal functions. Every other form of building on earth is a public house, a house for people to come together in for the fulfilment of social functions. Church, school, palace, mill, shop, post office, railway station, museum, art gallery, library, every kind of house except the home is a public house. These public houses are as essential to our social life and development as the private house is to our physical existence.

Inside the home are love, marriage, birth, and death; outside the home are agriculture, manufacture, trade, commerce, transportation, art, science, and religion. Every human—*i. e.*, social—process goes on outside the home, and has to have its appropriate building. In these varied forms of social activity, humanity finds its true expression; the contact and interchange, the stimulus and relief, without which the human soul cannot live.

Humanity *must* associate, that is the primal law of our being. This association, so far in history, has been almost entirely confined to men. They have associated in war, in work, in play. Men have always been found

[190]

in groups, on land and sea, doing things together; developing comradeship, loyalty, justice; enjoying the full swing of human faculties. But women, with the one partial exception of the privileges of the church, have been denied this most vital necessity of human life—association. Every woman was confined separately, in her private house, to her most separate and private duties and pleasures; and the duties and pleasures of social progress she was utterly denied. The church alone gave her a partial outlet; gave her a common roof for a common function, a place to come together in; and to the church she has flocked continually, as her only ground of human association.

But as society continued to evolve, reaching an ever-higher degree of interdependent complexity, developing in the human soul an ever-growing capacity and necessity for wide, free, general association, and transmitting that increasing social capacity to the daughter as well as the son, the enormous pressure had to find some outlet. " What will happen if an irresistible force meets an immovable body? " is the old question, and the answer is " The irresistible force will be resisted and the immovable body be moved." That is exactly what has happened. The irresistible force of the public spirit has met the immovable body of the private house—and that great, splendid, working social force has been frittered away in innumerable little processes of private amusement; the quiet, beautiful, private home has been bloated and coarsened in immeasurable distention as a place of public entertainment.

There is more than one line of tendency, good and bad, at work to bring about this peculiar phenomenon of domestic entertainment; but the major condition, without which it could not exist, is the home-bound woman; and the further essential, without which it could not develop to the degree found in what we call " society," is that the home-bound woman be exempt from the domestic industries, exempt from the direct cares of motherhood, exempt from any faintest hint of the great human responsibility of mutual labour; exempt from any legitimate connection with the real social body; and so, still inheriting the enormously increasing pressure of the social spirit, she pours out her energies in this simulacrum of social life we still call " social."

What is the effect, or rather what are some of the effects, of this artificial game of living upon the real course of life? And in particular how does it affect the home, and how does the home affect it? In the first place this form of human association, based upon the activities of otherwise idle women, and requiring the home as its vehicle of expression, tends to postpone marriage. The idle woman, contributing nothing to the household labours or expenses, requires to be wholly supported by her husband. This would be a check on marriage even if she stayed at home twirling her thumbs; for he would have to provide women to wait on her, on him, on the children, in default of her service as " housewife." He could not marry as soon as the man whose wife, strong and skilled in house-service, held up her end of the business, as does the farmer's and mechanic's wife to-day.

But when to the expense of maintaining a useless woman is added the expense of entertaining her useless friends; when this entertainment takes the form, not of hospitality sharing the accommodations of the home, the food of the family, but of providing extra rooms, furniture, dishes, and servants; of special elaboration of costly food; and of a whole new gamut of expensive clothing wherein to entertain and be entertained—then indeed does marriage recede, and youth wither and blacken in awaiting it.

Current fiction, current jokes, current experience, and all the background of history and literature, show us this strong and vicious tendency at work; and ugly is the work it does. No personal necessities, no family necessities, call for the expenses lavished on entertainment. Once started, the process races on, limited by no law of nature, for it is an unnatural process; excess following excess, in nightmare profusion. Veblen in his great book " The Theory of the Leisure Class," treats of the general development of this form of " conspicuous waste," but this special avenue of its maintenance is open to further study.

Women who work in their homes may be ignorant, uncultured, narrow; they may act on man as a check to mental progress; they may retard the development of their remaining industries and be a heavy brake on the wheels of social progress; they may and they do have this effect; but they are at least honest workers, though primitive ones. Their homes are held back from full social development, but they are legitimate homes. Their husbands, if selfish and vicious, waste money and life in the saloons, finding the social contact they must have somewhere; but the wives, getting along as they can without social contact, meet the basic requirements of home life, and offer to the honest and self-controlled young man a chance to enjoy " the comforts of a home," and to save money if he will. I am by no means pointing out this grade of woman's labour as desirable; that is sufficiently clear in previous chapters; but it is in origin right, and, though restricted, not abnormal.

Domestic entertainment is abnormal. It is an effort to meet a natural craving in an unnatural way. It continually seeks to " bring people together " because they are unnaturally kept apart; and to furnish them with entertainment in lieu of occupation. Any person whose work is too hard, too long, too monotonous, or not in itself attractive, needs " relaxation," " amusement," " recreation "; but this does not account in the least for domestic entertainment. That is offered to people who do not work at all. Those of them who do, part of the time, as business men sufficiently wealthy to be " in society," and yet sufficiently human to keep on in real social activities, are not relaxed, amused, or recreated by the alleged entertainment.

Those who most conspicuously and entirely give themselves up to it are most wearied by it. They may develop a morbid taste for the game, which cannot be satisfied without it; but neither are they satisfied within it.

The proofs of this are so patent to the sociologist as to seem tedious in enumeration; one alone carries weight enough to satisfy any questioner—that is the ceaseless and rapid contortions of invention with which the " entertainment " varies.

[195]

THE HOME

If the happy denizens of the highest " social circles " sat serene and content like the gods upon Olympus, banqueting eternally in royal calm, argument and criticism would fall to the ground. If they rose from their eternal banqueting, refreshed and strong, recreated in vigour and enthusiasm, and able to plunge into the real activities of life, then we might well envy them, and strive, with reason, to attain their level. But this is in no wise the case. Look for your evidence at the requisites of entertainment in any age of sufficient wealth and peace to maintain idlers, and in no age more easily typical than our own, and see the convulsive and inessant throes of change, the torrent of excess, the license, the eccentricity, the sudden reaction to this and that extreme, with which the wearied entertainers seek to devise entertainment that will entertain.

The physiologist knows that where normal processes are arrested abnormal processes develop. The persistent energy of the multiplying cell finds expression in cyst and polypus as readily as in good muscle and gland ; and, whereas the normal growth finds its natural limit and proportion in the necessary organic interchange with other working parts of the mechanism, no such healthy check acts upon the abnormal growth.

Legs and arms do not grow and stretch indefinitely,

putting out wabbling, pendulous eccentricities here and there; but a tumour grows without limit and without proportion; without use, and, therefore, without beauty. It takes no part in the bodily functions, and, therefore, is a disease. Yet it is connected with the body, grows in it, and swells hugely upon stolen blood. Social life has this possibility of morbid growth as has the physical body.

All legitimate social functions check and limit each other, as do our physical functions. No true branch of the social service can wax great at the expense of the others. If there are more in any trade or profession than are needed, the less capable are dropped out—cannot maintain a place in that line of work. Our use to each other is the natural check and guide in normal social growth. This whole field of domestic entertainment is abnormal in its base and direction, and therefore has no check in its inordinate expansion. As long as money can be found and brains be trained to minister to its demands the stream pours on; and all industry and art are corrupted in the service.

True social intercourse, legitimate amusement, is quite another matter. Human beings must associate, in innumerable forms and degrees of intimacy. Perfect friendship is the most intense, the closest form, and our great national and international organisations the largest and loosest. Between lies every shade of combination, temporary and permanent, deep and shallow, all useful and pleasant in their place. A free human being, rightly placed in society, has first his work—or her work —the main line of organic relation. That means special development, and all affiliations, economic and personal, that rest on that specialisation.

Then come the still larger general human connections, religious, political, scientific, educational, in which we join and work with others in the great world-functions that include us all. Play is almost as distinctively a human function as work—perhaps quite as much so; and here again we group and re-group, in sports and games, by " eights," by " nines," by " elevens," and all progressive associations. Then, where the play is so subtle and elaborate as to require a life's work, as in the great social function of the drama, we have people devoting their time to that form of expression, though they may seek their own recreation in other lines.

All natural mingling to perform together—as in the harvest dances and celebrations of all peoples—or to enjoy together the performance of others, as when we gather in the theatre, this is legitimate human life; and, while any one form may be overdeveloped, by excessive use, as an unwise athlete may misuse his body, it is still in its nature right, and good, if not misused.

But the use of the home as a medium of entertainment is abnormal in itself, in its relation, or, rather, in its total lack of relation to the real purpose of the place. The happy privacy of married love is at once lost. The quiet wisdom, peace, and loving care which should surround the child are at once lost. The delicate sincerity of personal expression, which should so unerringly distinguish one's dress and house, is at once lost. The only shadow of excuse for cumbering the home with crude industries— our claim that we do this so as to more accurately meet the needs of the family—is at once lost. The whole household machinery, once so nobly useful, and still interesting, as a hand-loom or spinning wheel, is prostituted to uses of which the primal home had no conception.

In an ideal home we should find, first, the perfect companionship of lovers; then the happy, united life of father, mother, and child, of brother and sister; then all simple, genuine hospitality; then the spontaneous intercourse of valued friends—the freedom to meet and mingle, now more, now less, in which, as character develops, we slowly find our own, and our whole lives are enriched and strengthened by right companionship.

Right here is the point of departure from the legitimate to the illegitimate; from what is natural, true, and wholly good to this avenue of diseased growth. As we reach out more and more for a wider range of contact—a chance of more varied association—we should leave the home and find what we seek in its own place: the general functions of human life, the whole wide field of human activity. In school, in college, the growing soul finds at once possibilities of contact impossible at home.

True association is impossible without common action. We do not sit voiceless and motionless, shaking hands with each other's souls. True and long-established friends and lovers may do this for a season. " Silence is the test of friendship," someone has said; but friendship and love require something more than this for birth and maintenance. The " ties " of love and friendship are found in the common memories and common hopes, the things we have done, do, and will do, for and with each other.

The home is for the family, and at most, a few " familiar " friends. The wider range of friendship, actual and potential, that the human soul of to-day requires, is not possible at home. See the broad graded

list of a man's school friends and college friends, class-
mates, and fellows in club and society, associates in
games and sports, business friends of all degrees, friends
and associates in politics; he has an enormous range of
social contact, from every grade of which he gets some
good, and, out of the whole, some personal friends he
likes to have come freely to his home.

Contrast with this the woman's scale—the average
woman, she whose " sphere " is wholly in the home. By
nature—that is, by human nature—she has the same
need and capacity for large association. Being pruned
down to a few main branches, confined almost wholly to
the basic lines of attachment known equally to the savage, she pours a passionate intensity of feeling into her
narrow range. The life-long give-and-take with a
friend of whose private life one knows nothing is impossible to her. She must monopolise, being herself
monopolised from birth.

This intensity of feeling, finally worn down by the
rebuff it must needs meet, gives place in the life of the
woman who is able to " entertain," to the " dear five
hundred friends " of that sterile atmosphere. It is
no longer the free reaching out of the individual toward
those who mean help and strength, breadth and change
and progress, rest and relaxation. In the varied life of

the world we are brought in contact with many kinds of people, in different lines of work, and are drawn to those who belong to us. In the monotonous life of " society " we are brought in contact with the same kind of people, or people whose life effort is to appear the same—all continually engaged in doing the same thing. If any new idea jars the monotony, off rushes the whole crowd after it—bicycle, golf, or ping-pong—till they have made it monotonous, too.

No true and invigorating social intercourse can take place among people who are cut off from real social activities, whose medium of contact is the utterly irrelevant and arbitrary performance of what they so exquisitely miscall " social functions." The foundation error lies in the confinement of a social being to a purely domestic scale of living. By bringing into the home people who have no real business there, they are instantly forced into an artificial position. The home is no place for strangers. They cannot work there, they cannot play there, so they must be " entertained." So starts the merry-go-round. The woman must have social contact, she cannot go where it is in the normal business of life, so she tries to drag it in where she is; forcing the social life into the domestic. The domestic life is crowded out by this foreign current, and, as there is no place for legitimate social activities, in any home or series of homes, however large and costly, the illegitimate social activities are at once set up.

The train of evils to the health of society we are all acquainted with, though not with their causes. Sociology is yet too new to us for practical application. We are too unfamiliar with normal social processes to distinguish the abnormal, even though suffering keenly under it. Yet this field is so within the reach of everyone that it would seem easy to understand.

The human being's best growth requires a happy, quiet, comfortable home; with peace and health, order and beauty in its essential relations. The human being also requires right social relation, the work he is best suited to, full range of expression in that work, and intercourse free and spontaneous with his kind. Women are human beings. They are allowed the first class of relations—the domestic; but denied the other—the social. Hence they are forced to meet a normal need in an abnormal way, with inevitable evil results.

We can see easily the more conspicuous evils of luxury and extravagance, of idleness, excitement, and ill health, of the defrauded home, the withering family life, the black shadows beyond that; but there are others we do not see. Large among these is our loneliness. The machinery of domestic entertainment is paradoxically in our way. We are for ever and for ever flocking together, being brought together, arranging to meet people, to be met by people, to have other people meet each other, and meanwhile life passes and we have not met.

"How I wish I could see more of you!" we sigh to the few real friends. Your friend may be at the same dinner—taking out someone else, or, even taking you out—in equal touch with neighbours at either side and eyes opposing. Your friend may be at the same dance—piously keeping step with many another; at the same reception, the same tea, the same luncheon—but you do not meet. As the "society" hand is gloved that there be no touching of real flesh and blood, so is the society soul dressed and defended for the fray in smooth phrase and glossy smile—a well-oiled system, without which the ceaseless press and friction would wear us raw, but within which we do anything but "meet."

For truth and health and honest friendliness, for the bringing out of the best there is in us, for the maintenance of a pure and restful home-life and the development of an inspiring and fruitful social life, we need some other medium of association than domestic entertainments. And we are rapidly finding it. The woman's club is a most healthy field of contact, and the woman's clubhouse offers a legitimate common ground for large gatherings.

The increasing number of women in regular business life alters the whole position. The business woman has her wider range of contact during the day, and is glad to rest and be alone with her family at night. If she desires to go out, it is to see real friends, or to some place of real amusement. When all women are honestly at work the " calling habit " will disappear perforce, with all its waste and dissimulation.

Given a healthy active life of true social usefulness for all women, and given a full accommodation of public rooms for public gatherings, and the whole thing takes care of itself. The enormous demand for association will be met legitimately, and the satisfied soul will gladly return from that vast field of social life to the restful quiet, the loving intimacy, the genuineness of home-life, with its constant possibilities of real hospitality and the blessings of true friendship.

XI

THE LADY OF THE HOUSE

THE effect of the house upon women is as important as might be expected of one continuous environment upon any living creature. The house varies with the varying power and preference of the owner; but to a house of some sort the woman has been confined for a period as long as history. This confinement is not to be considered as an arbitrary imprisonment under personal cruelty, but as a position demanded by public opinion, sanctioned by religion, and enforced by law.

In the comparative freedom to " walk abroad " of our present-day civilised women, we too quickly forget the conditions immediately behind us, when even the marketing for the household was done by men, and the conditions still with us for many millions of women in many countries who are house-bound for life.

To briefly recount the situation, we find in the prehuman home the mother sharing the hole or nest with her young, also sharing the outside task of getting food for them. In some species the father assists the mother, he never does it all. In other cases the father is no assistance, even a danger, seeking in cannibal infanticide to eat his own young; the mother in this case must feed and defend the young, as well as feed herself, and so must leave home at frequent intervals.

The common cat is an instance of this. She is found happily nursing the kittens in her hidden nest among the hay; but you often find the kittens alone while the mother goes mousing, and a contributary Thomas you do not find.

As we have before seen, our longer period of infancy and its overlapping continuity, a possible series of babies lasting twenty years or so, demanded a permanent home; and so long as the mother had sole charge of this progressive infant party she must needs be there to attend to her maternal duties. This condition is what we have in mind, or think we have in mind, when maintaining the duty of women to stay at home.

Wherever woman's labour is still demanded, as among all savages, in the peasant classes where women work in the fields, and in our own recent condition of slavery, either the mother takes her baby with her, or a group of babies are cared for by one woman while the rest are at work. Again, among our higher classes, almost the first step of increasing wealth is to depute to a nurse the mother's care, in order that she may be free from this too exacting claim. The nurse is a figure utterly unknown to animals, save in the collective creatures, like the bee and ant; a deputy-mother, introduced by us at a very early period. But this sharing of the mother's duties has not freed the woman from the house, because of quite another element in our human life. This is the custom of ownership in women.

The animal mother is held by love, by " instinct " only; the human mother has been for endless centuries a possession of the father. In his pride and joy of possession, and in his fear lest some other man annex his treasure, he has boxed up his women as he did his jewels, and any attempt at personal freedom on their part he considered a revolt from marital allegiance.

The extreme of this feeling results in the harem-system, and the crippled ladies of China; wherein we find the women held to the house, not by their own maternal ties, of which we talk much but in which we place small confidence, but by absolute force.

This condition modifies steadily with the advance of democratic civilisation, but the mental habit based upon it remains with us. The general opinion that a woman should be in the home is found so lately expressed as in the works of our present philosopher, Mr. Dooley. In

his " Expert Evidence " he says, " What the coort ought
to 've done was to call him up and say ' Lootgert, where's
your good woman? ' If Lootgert cudden't tell, he ought
to be hanged on gineral principles; f'r a man must keep
his wife around the house, and when she isn't there it
shows he's a poor provider."

The extent and depth of this feeling is well shown by
a mass of popular proverbs, often quoted in this connection, such as " A woman should leave her house three
times—when she is christened, when she is married, and
when she is buried " (even then she only leaves it to go
to church), or again, " The woman, the cat, and the
chimney should never leave the house." So absolute is
this connection in our minds that numbers of current
phrases express it, the Housewife—Hausfrau, and
the one chosen to head this chapter—The Lady of the
House.

Now what has this age-long combination done to the
woman, to the mother and moulder of human character;
what sort of lady is the product of the house?

Let us examine the physical results first. There is
no doubt that we have been whitened and softened by
our houses. The sun darkens, the shade pales. In the
house has grown the delicate beauty we admire, but are
we right in so admiring?

THE HOME

The highest beauty the world has yet known was bred by the sun-loving Athenians. Their women were home-bound, but their men raced and wrestled in the open air. No argument need be wasted to prove that air and sun and outdoor exercise are essential to health, and that health is essential to beauty. If we admire weakness and pallor, it by no means shows those qualities to be good; we can admire deformity itself, if we are taught to.

Without any reference to cause or necessity, it may be readily seen that absolute confinement to the house must have exactly the same effect on women that it would on men, and that effect is injurious to the health and vigour of the race. It is possible by continuous outdoor training of the boys and men to counteract the ill effect of the indoor lives of women; but why saddle the race with difficulties? Why not give our children strong bodies and constitutions from both sides?

The rapid and increasing spread of physical culture in modern life is helping mend the low conditions of human development; but the man still has the advantage.

This was most convincingly shown by the two statues made by Dr. Sargent for the World's Fair of 1893 from an extended series of measurements of college boys and girls. Thousands and thousands of specimens of our young manhood and young womanhood were carefully measured, and there stand the two white figures so show how we compare in beauty—the men and women of our time.

The figure of the man is far and away more beautiful than that of the woman. It is better proportioned as a whole; she is too short-legged, too long-waisted, too narrow-chested. It is better knit, more strongly and accurately " set up." She does not hang together well at all—the lines of connection are weak and wavering, and in especial does she lack any power and grace in the main area, the body itself, the torso. There is the undeveloped chest and the over-developed hips; and between them, instead of a beautifully modelled trunk, mere shapeless tissues, crying mutely for the arbitrary shape they are accustomed to put on outside! We are softer and whiter for our long housing; but not more truly beautiful.

The artist seeks his models from the stately burden-bearing, sun-browned women of Italy; strong creatures, human as well as feminine. The house life, with its shade, its foul air, its overheated steaminess, its innumerable tiring small activities, and its lack of any of those fine full exercises which built the proportions of the Greeks, has not benefited the body of the lady thereof; and in injuring her has injured all mankind, her children.

How of her mind? How has the mental growth of the race been affected by the housing of women? Apply the question to men. Think for a moment of the mental condition of humanity, if men too had each and every one stayed always in the home. The results are easy to picture. No enlargement of industry, only personal hand-to-mouth labour: not a trade, not a craft, not a craftsman on earth; no enlargement of exchange and commerce, only the products of one's own field, if the house-bound were that much free: no market, local, national, or international; no merchant in the world.

No transportation, that at once; *no roads*—why roads if all men stayed at home? No education—even the child must leave home to go to school; no art, save the squaw-art of personal decoration of one's own hand-made things. No travel, of course, and so no growth of any human ties, no widespread knowledge, love, and peace. In short, no human life at all—if men, all men, had always stayed at home. Merely the life of a self-maintained family—the very lowest type, the type we find most nearly approached by the remote isolated households of the " poor whites," of the South. Even they have some of the implements and advantages of civilisation, they are not utterly cut off.

The growth of the world has followed the widening lives of men, outside the home. The specialised trade, with its modification of character; the surplus production and every widening range of trade and commerce; the steadily increasing power of distribution, and transportation, with its increased area, ease, and speed; the ensuing increase in travel now so general and continuous; and following that the increase in our knowledge and love of one another; all—all that makes for civilisation, for progress, for the growth of humanity up and on toward the race ideal—takes place outside the home. This is what has been denied to the lady of the house— merely all human life!

Some human life she must needs partake of by the law of heredity, sharing in the growth of the race through the father; and some she has also shared through contact with the man in such time as he was with her in the house, to such a degree as he was willing and able to share his experience. Also her condition has been steadily ameliorated, as he, growing ever broader and wiser by his human relationships, brought wisdom and justice and larger love into his family relationship.

But the gain came from without, and filtered down to the woman in most niggardly fashion.

Literature was a great world-art for centuries and centuries before women were allowed to read—to say nothing of write! It is not long since the opinion was held that, if women were allowed to write, they would but write love letters! In our last century, in civilised Christian England, Harriet Martineau and Jane Austen covered their writing with their sewing when visitors came in; writing was " unwomanly! "

The very greatest of our human gains we have been the slowest to share with woman: education and democracy.

We have allowed them religion in a sense—as we have allowed them medicine—to take; not to give! They might have a priest as they might have a doctor, but on no account be one! Religion was for man to preach —and woman to practise.

In some churches, very recently, we are at last permitting women to hold equal place with men in what they deem to be the special service of God, but it is not yet common. Her extra-domestic education has been won within a lifetime; and there are still extant many to speak and write against it, even in the Universities— those men of Mezozoic minds! And her place as active

participant in democratic government is still denied by
an immense majority, on the ground—the same old
underlying ground—that it would take her from the
house! Here, clear and strong, stands out that ancient
theory, that the very existence of womanhood depends on
staying in the house.

We have seen what has been denied to woman by
absence from the world; what do we find bestowed upon
her by the ceaseless, enclosing presence of the house?
How does staying in one's own house all one's life affect
the mind? We cannot ask this question of a man, for
no man has ever done it except a congenital invalid.
Nothing short of paralysis will keep a man in the house.
He would as soon spend his life in petticoats, they are
both part of the feminine environment—no part of his.
He will come home at night to sleep, at such hours as
suit him. He likes to eat at home, and brings his friends
to see the domestic group—house, wife, and children;
all, things to be fond and proud of, things a man wishes
to own and maintain properly. But for work or play,
out he goes to his true companions—men, full-grown
human creatures who understand each other; in his true
place—the world, our human medium.

The woman, with such temporary excursions as our
modern customs permit, works, plays, rests, does all

[215]

things in her house, or in some neighbouring house—the same grade of environment. The home atmosphere is hers from birth to death. That this custom is rapidly changing I gladly admit. The women of our country and our time are marching out of the home to their daily work by millions, only to return to them at night with redoubled affection; but there are more millions far, many more millions, who are still housewives or ladies of houses.

The first result is a sort of mental myopia. Looking always at things too near, the lens expands, the focus shortens, the objects within range are all too large, and nothing else is seen clearly. To spend your whole time in attending to your own affairs in your own home inevitably restricts the mental vision; inevitably causes those same personal affairs to seem larger to you than other's personal affairs or the affairs of the nation.

This is a general sweeping consequence of being house-bound; and it is a heavily opposing influence to all human progress. The little-mindedness of the house-lady is not a distinction of sex. It is in no essential way a feminine distinction, but merely associatively feminine in that only women are confined to houses.

A larger range of interest and care instantly gives a resultant largeness of mind, in women as well as men.

THE LADY OF THE HOUSE

Such free great lives as have been here and there attained by women show the same broad human characteristics as similar lives of men. It can never be too frequently insisted upon, at least not in our beclouded time, that the whole area of human life is outside of, and irrelevant to, the distinctions of sex. Race characteristics belong in equal measure to either sex, and the misfortune of the house-bound woman is that she is denied time, place, and opportunity to develop those characteristics. She is feminine, more than enough, as man is masculine more than enough; but she is not human as he is human. The house-life does not bring out our humanness, for all the distinctive lines of human progress lie outside.

In the mind of the lady of the house is an arrangement of fact and feeling, which is untrue because it is disproportionate. The first tendency of the incessant home life is to exaggerate personality. The home is necessarily a hotbed of personal feeling. There love grows intense and often morbid; there any little irritation frets and wears in the constant pressure like a stone in one's shoe. The more isolated the home, the more cut off from the healthy movement of social progress, as in the lonely farmhouses of New England, the more we find those intense eccentric characters such as Mary E.

[217]

Wilkins so perfectly portrays. The main area of the mind being occupied with a few people and their affairs, a tendency to monomania appears. The solitary farmer is least able to escape this domestic pressure, and therefore we find these pathological conditions of home life most in scattered farms.

Human creatures, to keep healthy, *must* mingle with one another. The house-bound woman cannot; therefore she does not maintain a vigorous and growing mind. Such contact as she has is mainly through church opportunities; and along all such lines as are open to her she eagerly flocks, finding great relief therein. But compare the interchange between a group of house-ladies, and a corresponding group of men—their husbands perhaps. Each of these men, touching the world through a different trade, has an area of his own; from which he can bring a new outlook to the others. Even if all are farmers, in which case there is much less breadth and stimulus in their intercourse, they still have some connection with the moving world. They seek to meet at some outside point, the store, the blacksmith's shop, the railroad station, the post-office; the social hunger appeasing itself as best it may with such scraps of the general social activities as fall to it. But the women, coming together, have nothing to bring each other but personalities. Some slight variation in each case perhaps, a little difference in receipts for sponge-cake, cures for measles, patterns for clothes, or stitches for fancy-work. (Oh, poor, poor lives! where fancy has no work but in stitches, and no play at all!)

The more extended and well-supplied house merely gives its lady a more extended supply of topics of the same nature. She may discuss candle-shades instead of bed-quilts, " entrées " instead of " emptin's "; ferns for the table instead of " yarbs " for the garret; but the distinction is not vital. It is still the lady prattling of her circumambient house, as snails might (possibly do!) dilate upon the merits of their ever-present shells. The limitations of the house as an area for a human life are most baldly dreary and crippling in the lower grades, the great majority of cases, where the housewife toils, not yet become the lady of the house. Here you see grinding work, and endless grey monotony. Here are premature age, wasting disease, and early death. If a series of photographs could be made of the working housewives in our country districts, with some personal account of the " poor health " which is the main topic of their infrequent talk; we should get a vivid idea of the condition of this grade of house-bound life.

The lady is in a different class, and open to a different danger. She is not worn out by overwork, but weakened by idleness. She is not starved and stunted by the hopeless lack of expression, but is, on the contrary, distorted by a senseless profusion of expression. There is pathos even to tears in the perforated cardboard fly-traps dangling from the gaudy hanging lamp in the farmhouse parlour; the little weazened, withered blossom of beauty thrust forth from the smothered life below. There is no pathos, rather a repulsive horror, in the mass of freakish ornament on walls, floors, chairs, and tables, on specially contrived articles of furniture, on her own body and the helpless bodies of her little ones, which marks the unhealthy riot of expression of the overfed and underworked lady of the house.

Every animal want is met, save those of air and exercise, though nowadays we let her out enough to meet those, if she will do it in games and athletic sports— anything that has not, as Veblen puts it, " the slightest taint of utility." She is a far more vigorous lady physically, than ever before. Also, nowadays, we educate her; in the sense of a large supply of abstract information. We charge her battery with every stim- ulating influence during youth; and then we expect her to discharge the swelling current in the same peaceful circuit which contented her great-grandmother! This

THE LADY OF THE HOUSE

gives us one of the most agonising spectacles of modern times.

Here is a creature, inheriting the wide reach of the modern mind; that socially-developed mind begotten of centuries of broadest human intercourse; and, in our later years of diffused education, rapid transit, and dizzying spread of industrial processes, increasing its range and intensity with each generation. This tremendous engine, the healthy use of which requires contact with the whole field of social stimulus to keep up its supplies, and the whole field of social activity for free discharge, we expect to find peaceful expression in its own single house. There is of course a margin of escape—there must be.

In earlier decades the suppressed activity of this growing creature either still found vent in some refined forms of household industry, as in the exquisite embroideries of our grandmothers, or frankly boiled over in " society." The insatiate passion of woman for " society " has puzzled her unthinking mate. He had society, the real society of large human activities; but he saw no reason why she should want any. She ought to be content at home, in the unbroken circle of the family. While the real labours of the house held her therein she stayed, content or not; but, free of those, she has reached out widely in such planes as were open to her, for social contact. As women, any number of women, failed to furnish any other stimulus than that she was already overfilled with—they being each and all mere ladies of houses—she was naturally more attracted to the more humanly developed creature, man.

Man's power, his charm, for woman is far more than that of sex. It is the all-inclusive vital force of human life—of real social development. She has hung around him as devotedly as the cripple tags the athlete. When women have their own field of legitimate social activity, they retain their admiration for really noble manhood, but the " anybody, Good Lord! " petition is lost forever. A hint is perhaps suggested here, as to the world-old charm for women, of the priest and soldier. Both are forms of very wide social service—detached, impersonal, giving up life to the good of the whole— infinitely removed from the close clinging shadow of the house!

In our immediate time the progress of industry has cut the lady off from even her embroidery. Man, alert and inventive, follows her few remaining industries relentlessly, and grabs them from her, away from the house, into the mill and shop where they belong. But she, with ever idler hands, must stay behind. He will furnish her

THE LADY OF THE HOUSE

with everything her heart can wish—but she must stay right where she is and swallow it.

> *"Lady Love! Lady Love! wilt thou be mine?*
> *Thou shalt neither wash dishes, nor yet feed the swine!*
> *But sit on a cushion and sew a gold seam*
> *And feed upon strawberries, sugar, and cream!"*

This amiable programme, so exquisitely ludicrous, when offered to the world's most inherently industrious worker, becomes as exquisitely cruel when applied. The physical energies of the mother—an enormous fund—denied natural expression in bodily exertion, work morbidly in manifold disease. The social energies, boundless, resistless, with which she is brought more in contact every year, denied natural expression in world-service, work morbidly inside the painfully inadequate limits of the house.

Here we have the simple explanation of that unreasonable excess which characterises the lady of the house. The amount of wealth this amiable prisoner can consume in fanciful caprices is practically unlimited. Her clothing and ornament is a study in itself. Start any crazy fad or fashion in this field, and off goes the flood of self-indulgence, the craving for " expression," absrdity topping extravagance. There is nothing to check it save the collapse of the source of supplies.

A modern " captain of industry " has a brain so socially developed as to require for its proper area of expression an enormous range of social service. He gets it. He develops great systems of transportation, elaborate processes of manufacture, complex legislation or financial manœuvres. Without reference to his purpose, to the money he may acquire, or the relative good or evil of his methods, the point to be noted is that he is exercising his full personal capacity.

His sister, his wife, has a similar possibility of brain activity, and practically no provision for its exercise. So great is the growth, so tremendous the pressure of live brains against dead conditions, that in our current life of to-day we find more and more women pouring wildly out into any and every form of combination and action, good, bad, and indifferent. The church sewing circle, fair, and donation party no longer satisfy her. The reception, dinner, ball, and musicale no longer satisfy her. Even the splendid freedom of physical exercise no longer satisfies her. More and more the necessity for full and legitimate social activity makes itself felt; and more and more she is coming out of the house to take her rightful place in the world.

Not easily is this accomplished, not cheaply and safely. She is breaking loose from the hardest shell that ever held immortal seed. She is held from within by every hardened layer of untouched instinct which has accumulated through the centuries; and she is opposed from without by such mountain ranges of prejudice as would be insurmountable if prejudice were made of anything real.

The obsequious terror of a child, cowed by the nurse's bugaboo, is more reasonable than our docile acquiescence in the bonds of prejudice. It is pleasantly funny, knowing the real freedom so easily possible, to see a strong, full-grown woman solemnly state that she cannot pass the wall of cloudy grandeur with Mrs. Grundy for gate-keeper, that seems to hem her in so solidly. First one and then another reaches out a courageous hand against this towering barricade, touches it, shakes it, finds it not fact at all, but merely feeling—and passes calmly through. There is really nothing to prevent the woman of to-day from coming out of her old shell; and there is much to injure her, if she stays in.

The widespread nervous disorders among our leisure-class women are mainly traceable to this unchanging mould, which presses ever more cruelly upon the growing life. Health and happiness depend on smooth fulfilment of function, and the functional ability of a modern woman can by no means be exercised in this ancient coop.

The effect of the lady of the house upon her husband is worth special study. He thinks he likes that kind of woman, he stoutly refuses to consider any other kind; and yet his very general discontent in her society has been the theme of all observers for all time. In our time it has reached such prominence as to be commented upon even in that first brief halcyon period, the " honeymoon." *Punch* had a piteous cartoon of a new-married pair, sitting bored and weary on the beach, during their wedding journey. " Don't you wish some friend would come along? " said she. " Yes," he answered— " or even an enemy ! "

Men have accepted the insufficiencies and disagreeablenesses of " female society " as being due to " the disabilities of sex." They are not, being really due to the disability of the house-bound. Love may lead a man to " marry his housekeeper," and we condemn the misalliance; but he makes a housekeeper of his wife without criticism. The misalliance is still there.

A man, a healthy, well-placed man, has his position in the world and in the home, and finds happiness in both. He loves his wife, she meets his requirements as a husband, and he expects nothing more of her. His other requirements he meets in other ways. That she cannot give him this, that, and the other form of companionship, exercise, gratification, is no ground of blame; the world outside does that. So the man goes smoothly on, and when the woman is uncertain, capricious, exacting, he lays it to her being a woman, and lets it go at that.

But she, for all field of exertion, has but this house; for all kinds of companionship, this husband. He stands between her and the world, he has elected to represent it to her, to be " all the world " to her. Now, no man that ever lived, no series or combination of husbands that widowhood or polyandry ever achieved can be equivalent to the world. The man needs the wife and has her— needs the world and has it. The woman needs the husband—and has him; needs the world—and there is the husband instead. He stands between her and the world, with the best of intentions, doubtless; but a poor substitute for full human life.

" What else should she want? " he inquires in genuine amazement. " I love her, I am kind to her, I provide a good home for her—she has her children and she has me—what else should she want? "

What else does he want? He has her—the home and the children—does that suffice him? He wants also the human world to move freely in, to act fully in, to live widely in, *and so does she.*

And because she cannot have it, because he stands there in its stead, she demands of him the satisfaction of all these thwarted human instincts. She does not know what ails her. She thinks he does not love her enough; that if he only loved her enough, stayed with her enough, she would be satisfied. No man can sit down and love a woman eighteen hours a day, not actively. He does love her, all the time, in a perfectly reasonable way, but he has something else to do.

He loves her for good and all; it is in the bank, to draw on for the rest of life, a steady, unfailing supply; but she wants to see it and hear it and feel it all the time, like the miser of old who " made a bath of his gold and rolled in it."

The most glaring type of this unfortunate state of mind in recent fiction is that of the morbid Marna in the " Confessions of a Wife "—a vivid expression of what it is to be a highly-concentrated, double-distilled wife—*and nothing else!* No shadow of interest had she in life except this man; no duty, no pleasure, no use, no ambition, no religion, no business—nothing whatever but one embodied demand for her Man. He was indeed all the world to her—and he didn't like it.

THE LADY OF THE HOUSE

If the woman was fully developed on the human side she would cease to be overdeveloped on the feminine side. If she had her fair share of world-life she would expect of her husband that he be a satisfactory man, but not that he be a satisfactory world, which is quite beyond him. Cannot men see how deeply benefited they would be by this change, this growth of woman? She would still be woman, beautiful, faithful, loving; but she would not be so greedy, either for money or for love.

The lady of the house may be most softly beautiful, she may be utterly devoted, she may be unutterably appealing; but all her centuries of cherished existence have but brought us to *Punch's* "Advice to Those About to Marry": "Don't!"

The world's incessant complaint of marriage, mockery of marriage, resistance, outbreak, and default, gives heavy proof that that great human institution has serious defects. The blame has generally been laid on man. Suppose we now examine the other fact, the equal factor, and see if there is not some essential error in her position. This might furnish a wide field of study in the leisure hours of The Lady of the House.

XII

THE CHILD AT HOME

THERE are upon earth many millions of people—most of them children. Mankind has been continuous upon earth for millions of years; children have been equally continuous. Children constitute a permanent class, the largest class in the population. There are men, there are women, there are children, and the children outnumber the adults by three to two.

In the order of nature, all things give way before the laws and processes of reproduction; the individual is sacrificed to the race. Natural forces, working through the unconscious submission of the animal, tend steadily to improve a species through its young.

Social forces, working through our conscious system of education, tend to improve our species through its young. Humanity is developed age after age through a gradual improvement in its children; and since we have seen this and learned somewhat to assist nature by art, humanity develops more quickly and smoothly.

Every generation brings us more close to recognition

of this great basic law, finds us more willing to follow nature's principle and bend all our energies to the best development of the child. We early learned to multiply our power and wisdom by transmission through speech, and, applying that process to the child, we taught him what we knew, saving to humanity millennial periods of evolution by this conscious short-cut through education.

Nature's way of teaching is a very crude one—mere wholesale capital punishment. She kills off the erring without explanation. They die without knowing what for, and the survivors don't know, either. We, by education, markedly assist nature, transmitting quick knowledge from mouth to mouth, as well as slow tendency from generation to generation. More and more we learn to collect race-improvement and transmit it to the child, the most swift and easy method of social progress. To-day, more than ever before, are our best minds giving attention to this vital problem—how to make better people. How to make better bodies and better minds, better tendencies, better habits, better ideas—this is the study of the modern educator.

Slowly we have learned that the best methods of education are more in modifying influence than in transmitted facts; that, as the proverb puts it, " example is better than precept." The modifying influences of social environment have deeper and surer effect on the human race than any others, and that effect is strongest on the young. Therefore, we attach great importance to what we call the " bringing up " of children, and we are right. The education of the little child, through the influences of its early environment, is the most important process of human life.

Whatever progress we make in art and science, in manufacture and commerce, is of no permanent importance unless it modifies humanity for the better. That a race of apes should live by agriculture, manufacture, and commerce is inconceivable. They would cease to be apes by so living; but, *if they could*, those processes would be of no value, the product being only apes. We are here to grow, to become a higher and better kind of people. Every process of life is valuable in proportion to its contributing to our improvement, and the process that most contributes to our improvement is the most important of human life. That process is the education of the child, and that education includes all the influences which reach him, the active efforts of parent and teacher, the unconscious influence of all associates, and the passive effect of the physical environment.

All these forces, during the most impressionable years of childhood, and most of them during the whole period, are centered in the home. The home is by all means the most active factor in the education of the child. This we know well. This we believe devoutly. This we accept without reservation or inquiry, seeing the power of home influences, and never presuming to question their merit.

In our general contented home-worship we seem to think that a home—any home—is in itself competent to do all that is necessary for the right rearing of children. Or, if we discriminate at all, if we dare admit by referring to " a good home " that there are bad ones—we then hold all the more firmly that the usual type of " a good home " is the perfect environment for a child. If this dogma is questioned, our only alternative is to contrast the state of the child without a home to that of the child with one. The orphan, the foundling, the neglected child of the street is contrasted with the well-fed and comfortably clothed darling of the household, and we relapse into our profound conviction that the home is all right.

Again the reader is asked to put screws on the feelings and use the reason for a little while. Let us examine both the child and the home, with new eyes, seeing eyes, and consider if there is no room for improvement. And first, to soothe the ruffled spirit and quiet alarm, let it be here stated in good set terms that the author does NOT advocate " separating the child from the mother," or depriving it of the home. Mother and child can never be " separated " in any such sense as these unreasoning terrors suggest. The child has as much right to the home as anyone—*more*, for it was originated for his good. The point raised is, whether the home, as it now is, is the best and only environment for children, and, further, whether the home as an environment for children cannot be improved.

What is a child? The young of the human species. First, a young animal, whose physical life must be conserved and brought to full development. Then, a young human, whose psychical life, *the* human life, must be similarly cared for.

How does the home stand as regards either branch of development? In what way is it specifically prepared for the use, enjoyment, and benefit of a child? First, as to the structure of the thing, the house. We build houses for ourselves, modifying them somewhat according to climate, position, and so on. How do we modify them for children? What is there in the make-up of any ordinary house designed to please, instruct, educate, and generally benefit a child? In so far as he shares our own physical needs for shelter and convenience he is benefited; but, *as a child*, with his own specific necessities, desires, and limitations, what has the architect planned for the child—what have the mason and carpenter built for the child? Is there anything in the size and proportion, the material, the internal arrangement, the finish and decoration, to hint of the existence of children on earth?

The most that we find, in the most favoured houses, is " a sunny nursery." In one home of a thousand we find one room out of a dozen planned for children. What sort of an allowance is this for the largest class of citizens? Suppose our homes had, among the more expensive ones, one room for the adult family to flock into, and all the rest was built and arranged for children! We should think ourselves somewhat neglected in such an arrangement. But we are not as numerous as our children, nor as important; and, in any case, the home *belongs* to the child; he is the cause of its being; it is for him, hypothetically, that we marry and start a home.

What, then, is the explanation of this lack of special provision for the real founder of the home? This utter unsuitability of the house to the child, and the child to the house, finds its crowning expression in our cities, where house-owners refuse to let their houses to families with children! What are houses for? What are homes for? For children, first, last, and always! How, then, have we come to this vanishing point of absurdity? What paradoxical gulf stretches between these houses where " no children need apply " and the rest of the houses. *There is no visible difference in their plans and construction.* No houses are built for children; and these particular landlords simply accent the fact, and try to limit the use of the house to the persons for whom it was intended—the adults.

What is there in the presence of children in a house to alarm the owner? " They are so destructive," he will tell you; " they are mischievous, they are noisy. Other tenants object to them. They injure the house when old enough to run about, and squall objectionably when babies." All this is true enough. Most babies are a source of distress to their immediate neighbours because of their painful wailing, and most little children continue to cause distress by their noise in play and shrieks under punishment. Is all this outcry necessary? Must the poor baby suffer by night and day; must the small child bang and yell, and must it be punished so frequently? Why is the process of getting acclimated to the world so difficult and agonising? Is there really no way that the experience of all the ages may be turned to account to facilitate the first years of a child's life?

Our behaviour to the child rests on several assumptions

which are, at least, not proven. We assume that he has to be sick. We assume that he has to be naughty. We assume that life is hard and unpleasant, anyway, and that, the sooner he learns this and gets broken into it, the better. There is no more reason why a child should be sick than a calf or colt. Infancy is tender, and needs care, but it is not a disease. The Egyptian mother loves her baby, no doubt, though it goes blind through her ignorance and neglect—she knows nothing of ophthalmia, and lets the flies crawl over its helpless face, even while she loves it. We scorn and pity her ignorance, but we accept the colic, disorders of teething, and all the train of " preventable diseases " which kill off our babies, precisely as she accepts ophthalmia.

We have not learned yet how to make a baby the happy, contented, smoothly developing little animal that he should be. Some of us do better than others, but the knowledge of one is no gain to the rest, being confined to one family. Slowly the wider human care, the larger love, the broader knowledge, of doctor, nurse, and teacher are penetrating the innermost fortress of the home, and teaching the mother how to care for the child. The home did not teach her, and never would. In the untouched homes of ancient Eastern races, countless generations of mothers transmit the same traditional mistakes, love in the same blind way, and weep the same loss as unprofitably as they did ten thousand years ago.

In the homes of civilised races, where the light of social progress is most fully felt, we see the most improvement; but even here the pressure of growing knowledge is still combated by the jealous arrogance of the untaught mother, and the measureless inertia of the home.

In plain fact, what does the average home offer to the newcomer, the utterly defenceless baby, the all-important Coming Generation? See physical conditions first. To what sort of world is the new soul introduced? To a place built and furnished for several mixed and conflicting industries; not to a place planned for babies— aired, lighted, heated, coloured, and kept quiet to suit the young brain and body; but a building meant for a number of grown people to cook in, sweep and dust in, wash and iron in, cut and sew in, eat and wash dishes in, see their friends in, dress, undress, and sleep in; and incidentally, in the cracks and crevices of all these varied goings on, to " bring up " children in.

In that very small percentage of families where a nursery is arranged for children, and a nurse and a nursery-governess do deputy service for the always alleged " mother's care," we find some provision made

for children; but of what sort? This deputy is inferior
to the mother, save in a certain rule-of-thumb experience
which enables her to " manage children." Her knowledge of infant hygiene is not much greater, nor of
infant psychology. Look, for instance, at the babies of
our richer classes, as we see them continually in the
streets and parks. Our only alternative from the home
is the street, we having as yet no place for our babies.
If near a park so much the better, but in general the
sidewalk must serve, for rich or poor.

As one immediate physical condition, examine the dress
of these babies and young children; this among parents
of wealth, and, presumably, intelligence. See the baby
in the perambulator so rolled and bedded in, so tucked
and strapped, that he cannot move anything but perhaps
a stiffly projecting arm. Think of an adult cocooned in
this manner, unable to roll, stir, turn, in any way relieve
the pressure or change the attitude. And, when you
have considered the sensations of a tough and patient
adult frame, think further of those of a soft, tender,
active, and impatient baby body.

The dress of a baby or little child bears no relation
to his immediate comfort or to the needs of his incessant
growth. Among our wisest parents there is to-day a
new custom, happily increasing, of barefoot freedom, of

dirt-proof overalls, of a chance for beautiful, unconscious growth; but this does not reach the vast majority of suffering little ones. It does not spread because of the seclusion and irresponsible dominance of the separate home; and further—because of the low-grade intelligence of the home-bound mother.

She whose condition of arrested development makes her unquestioningly submit to the distortion, constriction, weight, and profusion of fashion in clothing for her own body, is not likely to show much sense in dressing a child. Beautiful fabrics, rich textures, expensive adornments, she heaps upon it. She wishes it to look pretty, according to her barbaric taste; and she disfigures the grave, sweet beauty of a baby face, the lovely moving curves of the little body, with heavy masses of stiff cloth, starched frippery, and huge, nodding, gaily decorated hats that would please an Ashantee warrior.

If some cartoonist would give us a copy of the Sistine Mother and Child in the costume of our mothers and children, showing those immortal cherub faces blinking obliquely from under flopping hat brims and rich plumes, perhaps we might in sudden shocked perception see with what coarse irreverence we disfigure our blessed little ones.

The child does not find in the home any assurance of

health, beauty, or free growth. He, and especially she, must wear the dainty garments on which our misguided mother love so wastefully lavishes itself; and must then be restricted in all natural exercise lest they be torn or soiled. To dress a little child so that he may be perfectly comfortable, and grow in absolute freedom, has not occurred to the home-bound mother.

Neither has she learned how to feed it. If the home is the best place for children, if the home is the best place for the preparation of food, would it not seem as if in all these long, long years we might have evolved some system of feeding little children so as to keep them at least alive—to say nothing of their being healthy?

The animal mother, guided by her unspoiled instinct, does manage to feed her young, and to teach it how to feed itself. The human mother, long since cut off from that poor primitive guidance, and proudly refusing to put knowledge in its place, feeds the baby in accordance with her revered domestic traditions, and calls in the doctor to remedy her mistakes. One man, in Buffalo, has recently saved fifteen hundred babies in a year, lowering the annual death rate by that amount, by public distribution of directions for preparing milk. He was not a mother. He was not shut up in a home. He studied and he taught in the light of public progress, in a growing world; and succeeded in filtering some of this saving knowledge into the darkness of fifteen hundred homes.

The average child is not fed properly; and there is nothing in the home to teach the mother how. She must learn outside, but she is not willing to. She still believes, and her husband with her, in the infallible power of " a mother's love " and " a mother's care "; and our babies are buried by thousands and thousands without our learning anything by the continual sacrifice. This is owing to the isolation of the home. If there were any general knowledge, general custom, association, comparison; if mothers considered their enormous responsibility *as a class*, instead of merely as individuals, this could not be. Knowledge and experience have to be gathered by wide and prolonged study; they do not come by an infinite repetition of the same private experiments.

We have to-day the first stirring of this great multitude of separately concealed experimenters toward that association and exchange of view, that carefully recorded observation, that reasonable study, which are necessary for any human advance. Our mothers are beginning to come out of their isolation into normal human contact; to take that first step toward wisdom—the acknowledgment of ignorance; and to study what little is known of this new science, Child-culture.

But it is only a beginning, very scant and small, and ridiculed unmercifully by the great slow dead-weight of the majority. The position of the satirist of modern motherhood is a safe and easy one. To ally one's self with the great mass of present humanity, and the far greater mass of the past, of all our hoary and revered traditions, and to direct this combined weight against the first movement of a new idea—this is an old game. Humanity has thus resisted every step of its own progress; but, though it makes that progress difficult and slow, it cannot wholly prevent it.

If the home and the home-bound mother do not ensure right food or clothing for the child, what do they offer in safety, and in the increasing educational influence which early environment must have? As to safety—the shelter of the home—we have already seen that even to the adult the home offers no protection from the main dangers of our time; disease, crime, and fire or other accident. The child not only shares these common dangers, but is more exposed to them, owing to more absolute confinement to the home and greater susceptibility. Whatever we suffer from sewer-gas, carbonic dioxide, or microbes and bacteria, the child suffers more.

THE HOME

He breathes the dust of our carpets, and eats it if we do not watch him. "I can't take my eyes off that child one minute," cries the admiring mamma, "or he'll be sure to put something in his mouth!" That a perfectly clean place might be prepared for a creeping baby, where there was nothing whatever he could put in his mouth, has never occurred to her. The child shares and more than shares every danger of the home, and furthermore suffers an endless list of accidents peculiar to his limitations. Even our dull nerves are roused to some sort of response by the terrible frequency of accidents to little children.

I have here a number, taken from one newspaper in one city during one year; not exhaustive daily scrutiny either; merely a casual collection:

"Mother and Baby Both Badly Burned." A three-year-old baby this—a match, a little night-dress flaming, struggle, torture, death! "Choked in Mother's Arms" is the next one; the divine instinct of Maternity giving a two-year-old child half a filbert to eat. It was remarked in the item that the "desolate couple" had lost two other little ones within two months. It did not state whether the two others were accidently murdered by a mother's care.

"Child's Game Proved Fatal" is the next. Three-

years-old twins were these; " playing fire engine in the
parlour while their mother prepared the midday meal."

One climbed on the table and lit a newspaper at a
gas jet, and set fire to the other. It is then related
"Both children cried out, but their mother, thinking they
were only playing, did not hasten to find what was the
matter." " The child died at 3 P. M." is the conclusion.

" Accidentally Killed His Baby " follows. The fond
father, holding his two-year-old son on his knee, shot and
killed him with a revolver " which he believed to be
empty."

" Escaping Gas Kills Baby "—" Boy Has Cent in
His Throat "—" Insane Mother's Crime "—" Drowns
her Eight-year-old Daughter "—and here a doctor says,
" It would be an excellent idea for every family to have a
little book giving briefly prompt antidotes for various
poisons. Physicians know that there are scores of cases
of accidental poisoning never heard of outside the family
concerned. I've had several cases of poisoning by an
accidental dose of chloroform and aconite liniment, and
one woman gave her child muriatic acid that was kept for
cleaning the marbles."

Another " Mother and Child Burned "—" Child
Scratched by a 60-foot Fall "—(this one was saved
by striking several clothes-lines after she fell out of the

window)—" Kitten was Life Preserver "—another fall out of a window, but the child was holding a kitten, and her head struck on it—so only the kitten was smashed.

" A Governor's Child badly Hurt "—" will probably prove fatal," this was a two-story drop over a staircase; and shows that it is not only in the homes of the poor that these things happen. Another " Baby Burned " follows—this poor little one was left strapped into its carriage, and set fire to by an enterprising little brother.

" Tiny Singer Fell Dead " describes a five-year-old boy as singing a selection from " Cavalleria Rusticana " as a means of entertaining a party of young friends— and burst a blood-vessel in the brain. Then there is a story of a grisly murder in which a tiny child testifies as to seeing her father kill her mother; the child was not hurt—physically. And then a bit of negative evidence quite striking in its way, describing " The Mother of Twenty-five Children " and incidentally stating " of these only three sons and four daughters are now living." Seven out of twenty-five does not seem a large proportion to survive the perils of the home.

These are a few, a very few, instances of extreme injury and death. They are as nothing to the wide-spread similar facts we do not hear of; and as less than nothing to the list of minor accidents to which little children are constantly exposed in the shelter of the home. We bar our windows and gate our stairs in some cases; but our principal reliance is on an unending watchfulness and a system of rigid discipline. " Children need constant care! " we maintain; and " A child must be taught to mind instantly, for its own protection." A child is not a self-acting poison or explosive. If he were in an absolutely safe place he might be free for long, bright, blessed hours from the glaring Argus-eyed watchfulness which is so intense an irritant. Convicts under sentence of death are in their last hours kept under surveillance like this, lest they take their own lives. Partly lest the child injure himself among the many dangers of the home, and partly lest he injure its frail and costly contents, he grows up under " constant watching." If this is remitted, he " gets into mischief " very promptly. " Mischief " is our broad term for the natural interaction of a child and a home. The inquiry of the young mind, and the activity of the young body, finding no proper provision made for them, inevitably fall foul of our complicated utensils, furniture, and decorations, and what should be a normal exercise becomes " mischief."

Our chapter of accidents here leads us to the great underlying field of education. Say that the child lives to grow up, during these wholly home-bound years; in spite of wrong clothing, wrong feeding, and the many perils we fatuously call " incident to babyhood " (when they are only incident to our lack of proper provision for babyhood). If he battles through his infancy and early childhood successfully, what has he gained from his early environment in education? What are the main facts of life, as impressed upon every growing child by his home surroundings?

The principal fact is eating. This he learns perforce by seeing his mother spending half her time on that one business; by seeing so much house-space given to it; by the constant arrival of food supplies, meat, groceries, milk, ice, and the rest; and excursions to get them. The instincts of early savagery, which every child has to grow through, are heavily reinforced by the engrossing food-processes of the home.

They do not necessarily please him or her, either. The child does not grow up with a burning ambition to be a cook. Whether the ever-present kitchen business was run by the mother or by a servant, it was not run joyously and proudly; nor was it run in such wise as to really teach the child the principles of hygiene in food-values and preparation. If the family is a wealthy one the child is not allowed in the kitchen perhaps, but is the more impressed by the complicated machinery of the dining-room, and that elaborate cult of special " manners " used in this sacred service of the body. Thus and thus must he eat, and thus handle his utensils; and if the years and the tears spent in acquiring these Eleusinian mysteries make due impression on the fresh brain tissue, then we may expect to find the human being more impressed by the art of eating than by any other.

And so we do find him. The children of the kitchen are differently affected from the children of the dining-room. These last, of our " upper classes," receive the indelible stamp of the tri-daily ritual, and go through the rest of life thinking more highly of " table manners " than of any other line of conduct, for the reason that they were more incessantly, thoroughly, and importunately taught that code than any other. To handle a fork properly is insisted upon far more imperatively than to properly handle a temper.

The principal business of the home being the care of the body, and this accomplished through these archaic domestic industries, the unending up-current of young life, which should so steadily purify and uplift the world, in every generation is steeped anew in this exaggeration of physical needs and caprices.

Beyond the overwhelming cares of the table the other

home industries involve the care and replenishment of furniture and clothes. Hour after hour, day after day, the child sees his mother devoting her entire life to attendance upon these things—the daily cleaning, the weekly cleaning, the spring and fall cleaning, the sewing and mending at all times.

These things must be done, by some people, somewhere; but must they be done by all people, that is by all women, the people who surround the child, and all the time? Must the child always associate womanhood with house-service; and assume, necessarily assume, that the main business of life is to be clean, well-dressed, and eat in a proper manner?

If the mother is not herself the house-servant—what else is she? What does the growing brain gather of the true proportions of life from his dining-room-and-parlour mamma? Her main care, and talk, is still that of food and clothes; and partly that of " entertainment," which means more food and more clothes.

Can we not by one daring burst of effort imagine a home where there was still the father and mother love, still the comfort, convenience, and beauty we so enjoy, still the sweet union of the family group, and yet no kitchen? Perhaps even, in some remote dream, no dining-room? Where the mother was a wise, strong, efficient human being, interested in and working for the progress of humanity; and giving to her baby, in these sweet hours of companionship, some true sense of what life is for and how it works. No, we cannot imagine it, most of us. We really cannot. We are so indelibly kitchen-bred, or dining-room-bred, that mother means cook, or at least housekeeper, to our minds; and family means dinner-table.

So grows the child in the home. In the school he learns something of social values, in the church something, in the street something; from his father, who is a real factor in society, something; but in the home he learns by inexorably repeated impressions of every day and hour, that life, this deep, new, thrilling mystery of life consists mainly of eating and sleeping, of the making and wearing of clothes. We are irresistibly reminded of the strange text, " Take no thought of what ye shall eat or what ye shall drink or wherewithal ye shall be clothed." A little difficult to follow this command when mother does nothing else!

XIII

THE GIRL AT HOME

WHAT is the position of the home toward us in youth? We have seen something of its effect upon the child, the wholly helpless child, who knows no other place or power. We have seen something of its effect upon the woman in her life-long confinement there. Between childhood and maturity comes youth; holding what is left of the child's pure heart and vivid hopes, and what begins to stir of man's or woman's power. The gain of a race, if there is a gain, must make itself felt in youth—more strength, more growth, more beauty, a larger conscience, a sounder judgment, a more efficient will.

Each new generation must improve upon its parents; else the world stands still or retrogrades. In this most vivid period of life how does the home meet the needs of the growing soul? The boy largely escapes it. He is freer, even in childhood; the more resistant and combative nature, the greater impatience of pain, makes the young male far harder to coerce. He sees his father always going out, and early learns to view the home from a sex-basis, as the proper place for women and children, and to push incessantly to get away from it.

From boy to boy in the alluring summer evenings we hear the cry, " Come on out and have some fun ! " Vainly we strive and strive anew to " keep the boys at home." It cannot be done. Fortunately for us it cannot be done. We dread to have them leave it, and with good reason, for well we know there is no proper place for children in the so long unmothered world ; but even in danger and temptation they learn something, and those who struggle through their youth unscathed make better men than if they had been always softly shielded in the home.

The world is the real field of action for humanity. So far humanity has been well-nigh wholly masculine ; and the boy, feeling his humanity, pushes out into his natural field, the world. He learns and learns, from contact with his kind. He learns about all sorts of machinery, all manner of trades and businesses. He has companions above him and below him and beside him, the wide human contact in which we grow so rapidly. If he is in the city he knows the city, if he is in the country he knows the country, far more fully than his sister. A thousand influences reach him that never come to her, formative influences, good and bad, that modify character. He has far less of tutelage, espionage, restraint; he has more freedom by daylight, and he alone has any freedom after dark. All the sweet, mysterious voices of the night, the rich, soft whisperings of fragrant summer, when the moon talks and the young soul answers; the glittering, keen silence of winter nights, when between blue-black star-pointed space and the level shine of the snow stands but one living thing—yourself—all this is cut off from the girl. The real intimacy with nature comes to the soul alone, and the poor, over-handled girl soul never has it.

In some few cases, isolated and enviable, she may have this common human privilege, but not enough to count. She must be guarded in the only place of safety, the home. Guarded from what? From men. From the womanless men who may be prowling about while all women stay at home. The home is safe because women are there. Out of doors is unsafe because women are not there. If women were there, everywhere, in the world which belongs to them as much as to men, then everywhere would be safe. We try to make the women safe in the home, and keep them there; to make the world safe for women and children has not occurred to us. So the boy grows, in the world as far as he can reach it, and the girl does not grow equally, being confined to the home. In very recent years, within one scant century, we are letting the girls go to school, even to college. They pour out into the larger field and fill it at once. Their human faculties have some chance to grow as well as the over-emphasised feminine ones; and in our schools and colleges youth of both sexes finds the room, stimulus, and exercise it could not find at home.

The boy who does not go to college goes to business, to work in some way. To find an able-bodied intelligent boy in a home between breakfast and supper would argue a broken leg. But girls we find by thousands and thousands; " helping mother," if mother does the work; and if there are servants to do the work, the girl does— what?

What is the occupation of the daughter of the house? Let us suppose her to be healthy. Let us suppose her to have a fair share of ability and education. She has no longer the school or the college, she has only the home. Not that she is physically confined there. She may go out by daylight, giving careful account of her steps, and visit other girls in their homes. She may receive visits, both from girls and boys; and she may go out continually to all manner of entertainments. Perhaps she is expected to dust the parlour, to arrange the flowers, to " keep up her music." She has enough to eat, enough and more than enough to wear; but what exercise has she for body or brain? Perhaps in games and dances she keeps her body active—but what sort of occupation is that for a young human creature of this century, a creature of power? The young woman has the same race inheritance of ability, the same large brain-growth, as the man. The physical improvement of our times is reflected in them too; fine stalwart girls we see, tall, straight, broad-shouldered. She has had, in specific education, the same mental training as the boy.

How would her brother be content with a day's work of dusting the parlour and arranging the flowers; of calling and being called on? Amusement is good, sometimes necessary; best and most necessary to the tired, unhappy, and overworked. But youth—healthy, happy, and vigorous, full of the press of unused power and the accumulating ambition of all the centuries—why should youth waste its splendour in such unsatisfying ways?

If you ask the father, he will merely say that it is the proper position for a girl; he is " able to support her," she does not " have to work," she can amuse herself, and as for a field for her abilities—she will find that in her own home when she is married. Ask her mother—and she will tell you, making a sad confession all unknowingly —" let her enjoy herself now; she will have care enough later." There is a tacit agreement that girls shall have all the " good time " possible while they are girls, that they may have it to remember! Does this " good time " satisfy the girl? Is she happy in her father's home, just passing the time till she moves into her husband's?

Sometimes she is. Her education has been strong to make her so. The home atmosphere of predominant clothes and food has been about her from the cradle, and she still has clothes and food, and may elaborate them without limit. She may devote as much time to the adornment of the table as she wishes; and if her inclination take her also to the kitchen, perhaps even to the cooking school, that is more than well. She may also devote herself to the parlour and its adornment; but most naturally of all to the adornment of her own young body—all these are proper functions of the home. She may love and serve her immediate dear ones also, to any extent; that is the basic principle of it all, that is occupation enough for any girl. Yes, there is occupation enough as far as filling time goes; but how if it does not satisfy? How if the girl wants something else to do—something definite, something developing?

This is deprecated by the family. " Work " is held by all to be a thing no mortal soul should do unless compelled by want. We speak sadly, tenderly, of the poor girl whose father died and left her unprovided for, wherefore " she had to work." We have not learned to see that some kind of work is necessary to all human creatures to use their powers; not mere tread-mill repetition of small, useless things, but such range of action as shall exercise all the faculties. And least of all have we learned to see that a human soul, to be healthy, must love and care for more than its own blood relations.

What the girl, as a normal human being, wants is full exercise in large social relation; things to think about, feel, and do, which do not in any way concern the home. Race-babyhood may be content at home—it was first made for babies. But as we grow up into our modern human range of power, no home can or ought to content us. We need not, therefore, cease to love it, need not neglect or ignore it. We simply need something more. That is the great lack which keeps girlhood unsatisfied; the call of the human soul for its full field of action, the world. We try to meet this lack by a surfeit of supplies for lower needs.

Since we first began to force upon our girl baby's astonished and resisting brain the fact that she was a girl; since we curbed her liberty by clothing and ornament calculated only to emphasise the fact of sex, and by restrictions of decorum based upon the same precocious distinction, we have never relaxed the pressure. As if we feared that there might be some mistake, that she was not really a girl but would grow up a boy if we looked the other way, we diligently strove to enforce and increase her femininity by every possible means. So by the time her womanhood does come it finds every encouragement, and the humanhood which should predominate we have restricted and forbidden. Moreover, whatever of real humanness she does manifest we persist in regarding as feminine.

For instance, the girl wants friends, social contact. She cannot satisfy this want in normal lines of work, in the natural contact of the busy world, so she tries to meet it on the one plane allowed—in what we call "Society." Her own life being starved, she seeks to touch other lives as far and fast as possible. Next to doing things one's self is the association with others who can do them. So the girl reaches out for friends. Women friends can give her little; their lives are empty as her own, their talk is of the same worn themes— their point of view either the kitchen or the parlour. Therefore she finds most good in men friends; they are human, they are doing something. All this is set down to mere feminine " desire to attract "; we expect it, and we provide for it. Our " social " machinery is largely devoted to " bringing young people together "; not in any common work, in large human interests, but in such decorated idleness, with music, perfume, and dance, as shall best minister to the only forces we are willing to promote.

Is the girl satisfied? Is it really what she wants, all she wants? If she were a Circassian slave, perhaps it would do. For the daughter of free, active, intelligent, modern America it does not do; and therefore our girls in ever-increasing numbers are leaving home. It is not that they do not love their homes; not that they do not want homes of their own in due season; it is the protest of every healthy human soul against the-home-and-nothing-else.

Our poorer girls are going into mills and shops, our richer ones into arts and professions, or some educational and philanthropic work. We oppose this proof of racial growth and vitality by various economic fallacies about " taking the bread out of other women's mouths "—and in especial claim that it is " competing with men," " lowering wages " and the like. We talk also, in the same breath, or the next one, about " the God-given right to work "—and know not what we mean by that great phrase.

To work is not only a right, it is a duty. To work

to the full capacity of one's powers is necessary for human development. It is no benefit to a human being to keep him, or her, in down-wrapped idleness, it is a gross injury. If a man could afford to put daughters and wife to bed and have them fed and washed like babies, would that be a kindness? "They do not have to walk!" he might say. Yes, they do have to, else would their muscles weaken and shrink, and beauty and health disappear. For the health and beauty of the body it must have full exercise. For the health and beauty of the mind it must have full exercise. No normal human mind can find full exercise in dusting the parlour and arranging the flowers; no, nor in twelve hours of nerve-exhaustion in the kitchen. Exhaustion is not exercise.

"But they are free to study—to read, to improve their minds!" we protest. Minds are not vats to be filled eternally with more and ever more supplies. It is *use*, large, free, sufficient use that the mind requires, not mere information. Our college girls have vast supplies of knowledge; how can they use it in the home? Could a college boy apply his education appropriately to "keeping house"—and, if not, how can the girl? Full use of one's best faculties—this is health and happiness for both man and woman.

THE HOME

But how about those other people's wages?—will be urged. Productive labour adds to the wealth of the world, it does not take away. If wealth were a fixed quantity, shared carefully among a lot of struggling beggars, then every new beggar would decrease the other's share.

To work is to *give*, not to beg. Every worker adds to the world's wealth, increases everyone's share. Of course there are people whose " work " is not of value to anyone; who simply use their power and skill to get other people's money away from them; the less of these the better. That is not productive labour. But so long as we see to it that the work we do is worth more than the pay we get, our consciences may be clean; we give to the world and rob no one. As to the immediate facts that may be alleged, " overcrowded labour market," " overproduction," and such bugaboos, these are only facts as watered stock and stolen franchises are facts; not economic laws, but criminal practices. A temporary superficial error in economic conduct need not blind us to permanent basic truth, and the truth which concerns us here is that a human creature must work for the health and power and pleasure of it; and that all good work enriches the world.

So the girl need not stay at home and content her soul

with chocolate drops lest some other girl lose bread. She may butter that bread and share the confections, by her labour, if it be productive. And by wise working she may learn to see how unwise and how unnecessary are the very conditions which now hold her back. At present she is generally held back. Her father will not allow her to work. Her mother needs her at home. So she stays a while longer. If she marries, she passes out of this chapter, becoming, without let or change, " the lady of the house." If she does not marry, what then? What has father or mother, sister or brother, to offer to the unmarried woman? What is the home to her who has no " home of her own "?

The wife and mother has a real base in her home: distorted and overgrown . though it may have become, away in at the centre lies the everlasting founder—in the little child. Unnecessary as are the mother's labours now, they were once necessary, they have a base of underlying truth. But what real place has a grown woman of twenty-five and upwards in anyone's else home? She is not a child, and not a mother. The initial reason for being at home is not there. What business has she in it? The claim of filial devotion is usually advanced to meet this question. Her parents need her. And here comes out in glaring colours the distinction between girl and boy, between man's and woman's labour.

Whatever of filial gratitude, love, and service is owed to the parent is equally owed by boy and girl. If there is a difference it should be on the boy's side, as he is more trouble when little and less assistance in the house when big. Now, what is the accepted duty of the boy to the parents, when they are old, feeble, sick, or poor? First, to maintain them, that is, to provide for them the necessaries of life and as much more as he can compass. Then, to procure for them service and nursing, if need be. Also himself to bestow affection and respect, and such part of his time as he can spare from the labour required to maintain them. This labour he performs like a civilised man, by the service of other people in some specialised industry; and his ability to care for his parents is measured by his ability to perform that larger service.

What is the accepted duty of the girl to the parents in like case? She is required to stay at home and wait upon them with her own hands, serve them personally, nurse them personally, give all her time and strength to them, and this in the old, old uncivilised way, with the best of intentions, but a degree of ability measured by the lowest of averages.

THE GIRL AT HOME

It is the duty of the child to care for the infirm parent —that is not questioned; but how? Why, in one way, by one child, and in so different a way by another? The duty is precisely the same; why is the manner of fulfilling it so different? If the sick and aged mother has a capable son to support her, he provides for her a house, clothing, food, a nurse, and a servant. If she has but a daughter, that daughter can only furnish the nurse and servant in her own person, skilled or unskilled as the case may be; and both of them are a charge upon the other relatives or the community for the necessaries of life. Why does not the equally capable daughter *do more* to support her parent when it is necessary? She cannot, if she is herself the nurse and servant. Why does she have to be herself the nurse and servant? Because she has been always kept at home and denied the opportunity to take up some trade or profession by which she could have at once supported herself, her parents, and done good service in the world. Because " the home is the place for women," and in the home is neither social service nor self-support.

There is another and a darker side to this position. The claim of exclusive personal service from the daughter is maintained by parents who are not poor, not old, not sick, not feeble; by a father who is quite able to

[265]

pay for all the service he requires, and who prefers to maintain his daughter in idleness for his own antiquated masculine pride—and by a mother who is quite able to provide for herself, if she choose to ; who is no longer occupied by the care of little children, who does not even do house-service, but who lives in idleness herself, and then claims the associate idleness of her daughter, on grounds past finding out. Perhaps it is that an honourably independent daughter, capable, respected, well-paid, valuable to the community, would be an insupportable reproach to the lady of the house. Perhaps it is a more pathetic reason—the home-bound, half-developed life, released from the immediate cares, which, however ill-fulfilled, at least gave sanction to her position, now seeks to satisfy its growing emptiness by the young life's larger hope and energy. This may be explanation, but is no justification.

The value and beauty of motherhood depend on the imperative needs of childhood. The filial service of the child depends on the imperative needs of the parent. When the girl is twenty-one and the mother is forty-five, neither position holds. The amount of love and care needed by either party does not require all day for its expression. The young, strong, well-educated girl should have her place and work, equally with her brother.

THE GIRL AT HOME

Does not the mother love her son, though he is in business? Could she not manage to love a daughter in business, too? It is not love, far less is it wisdom, which so needlessly immolates a young life on the altar of this ancient custom of home-worship. The loving mother is not immortal. What is to become of the unmarried daughter after the mother is gone?

What has the home done to fit her for life. She may be rich enough to continue to live in it, not to " have to work," but is she, at fifty, still to find contentment in dusting the parlour and arranging the flowers, in calling and receiving calls, in entertaining and being entertained? Where is her business, her trade, her art, her profession, her place in life? The home is not the whole of life. It is a very minor part of it—a mere place of preparation for living. To keep the girl at home is to cut her off from life.

More and more is this impossible. The inherited power of the ages is developing women to such an extent that by the simple force of expansion they are cracking the confining walls about them, bursting out in all directions, rising under the enormous pressure that keeps them down like mushrooms under a stone. The girl has now enough of athletic training to strengthen her body, balance her nerves, set her tingling with the healthy impulse to *do*. She has enough mental training to give some background and depth to her mind, with the habit of thinking somewhat. If she is a college girl, she has had the inestimable privilege of looking at the home *from outside*, in which new light and proportion it has a very different aspect.

The effort is still made by proud and loving fathers, unconscious of their limitations, to keep her there afterward, and by loving mothers even more effectually. They play upon the strings of conscience, duty, and affection. They furnish every pleasant temptation of physical comfort, ease, the slow corruption of unearned goods. To oppose this needs a wider range of vision and a greater strength of character than the daughter of a thousand homes can usually command.

The school has helped her, but she has not had it long. The college has helped her more, but that is not a general possession as yet, and has had still shorter influence. Strong, indeed, is the girl who can decide within herself where duty lies, and follow that decision against the combined forces which hold her back. She must claim the right of every individual soul to its own path in life, its own true line of work and growth. She must claim the duty of every individual soul to give to its all-providing society some definite service in return. She must recognise the needs of the world, of her country, her city, her place and time in human progress, as well as the needs of her personal relations and her personal home. And, further, using the parental claim of gratitude and duty in its own teeth, she must say: " Because I love you I wish to be worthy of you, to be a human creature you may be proud of as well as a daughter you are fond of. Because I owe you care and service when you need it, I must fit myself now to render that care and service efficiently. Moreover, my duty to you is not all my duty in the world. Life is not merely an aggregation of families. I must so live as to meet all my duties, and, in so doing, I shall better love and serve my parents."

Conscience is strong in women. Children are very violently taught that they owe all to their parents, and the parents are not slow in foreclosing the mortgage. But the home is not a debtor's prison—to girls any more than to boys. This enormous claim of parents calls for examination.

Do they in truth do all for their children; do their children owe all to them? Is nothing furnished in the way of safety, sanitation, education, by that larger home, the state? What could these parents do, alone, in never so pleasant a home, without the allied forces of society to maintain that home in peace and prosperity. These lingering vestiges of a patriarchal cult must be left behind. Ancestor-worship has had victims enough. Girls are human creatures as well as boys, and both have duties, imperative duties, quite outside the home.

One more protest is to be heard: "Most girls marry. Surely they might stay at home contentedly until they leave it for another." Yes, most girls marry. All girls ought to—unless there is something wrong with them. And, being married, they should have homes. But, to have a home and enjoy it, is one thing; to stay in it—the whole time—is quite another. It is the same old assumption that woman is a house-animal; that she has no place in the open, no business in the world. If the girl had a few years of practical experience in the world she would be far better able to enjoy and appreciate her own home when she had one. At present, being so much restricted where she is, she very often plunges from the frying-pan into the fire, simply from too much home.

"Why should she have married that fellow!" cries the father; "I gave her a good home—she had everything she wanted." It does not enter the mind of this man that a woman is something more than a rabbit. Even rabbits, well-fed rabbits, will gnaw and dig to get out—they like to run as well as eat. Also, the girl whose character has time to " set " a little in some legitimate business associations, instead of being held in everlasting solution at home, will be able to face the problems of domestic industry and expense with new eyes.

No men, with practical sense and trained minds, would put up for a week with the inchoate mass of wasted efforts in the home; and, when women have the same trained minds and practical sense, they will not put up with it much longer. For the home's sake, as well as her own sake, the girl will profit by experience in the working world.

Once she learns the pleasure and power of specialisation, the benefits of organisation, the advantages of combination, the whole tremendous enginery of civilised life, she can no more drop back into her ancestral cradle than her brother could turn into an Arcadian shepherd, piping prettily to his fleecy charge.

XIV

HOME INFLUENCE ON MEN

IN our peculiar and artificial opposition of " the
Home " and " the World," we have roughly
ascribed all the virtues to the first, and all the vices
to the second. " The world, the flesh, and the devil "
we still associate, forgetting that home is the very
temple of the flesh, and in no way impervious to the
devil. Sin is found at home as generally as elsewhere—
must be, unless women are sinless and men absolved on
entering the sacred door.

There are different sins and virtues, truly, as we have
seen in the chapter on Domestic Ethics. There is less
fighting at home, as there is but one man there. There
is less stealing, the goods being more in common, only
sometimes a sly rifling of pockets by the unpaid wife.
A man pays his housekeeper, or his housemaids, because
he has to ; and he pays, and pays highly, the purely ex-
tortionate women of pleasure ; but sometimes he forgets
to pay his wife, and sometimes she steals. The home
has patience, chastity, industry, love. But there is
less justice, less honour, less courage, less truth ; it

does not embrace all the virtues. Such as it is, strong for good and also very weak for some good, possibly even showing some tendencies to evil, what is its influence on men?

The boy baby feels it first; and that we have touched on. The home teaches the boy that women were made for service, domestic service, that the principal cares and labours of life are those which concern the body, and that his own particular tastes and preferences are of enormous importance. As fast as he gets out of the home and into the school, he learns quite other things, getting his exaggerated infant egotism knocked out of him very suddenly, and, as he gets out of school and into business, also into politics, he learns still further of the conditions of life. Proportion changes, perspective changes; he grows to have a very different view of life from the woman's view. The same thing happening to a man and a woman produces a widely varying effect; what is a trifle in the day's large activities to him is an event of insistent pressure to her; and, here, in the eternal misunderstanding between the home-bred woman and the world-bred man, lie the seeds of ceaseless trouble. The different range of vision of the occupant of the home and the occupant of the world makes it impossible for them to see things similarly. We are familiar with the difference, but have always considered it a distinction of sex.

We have called the broader, sounder, better balanced, more fully exercised brain " a man's brain," and the narrower, more emotional and personal one " a woman's brain "; whereas the difference is merely that between the world and the house. The absolute relation between any animal's brain and his range of activity is patent to the zoölogist, and simply furnishes the proof of its law of development. The greater the extent and complexity of any creature's business, the greater the mental capacity, of course.

We are familiar with the mental effect of living on small islands—" the insular mind," " insular prejudice " are well known terms. The smaller the island, the more deprived of contact and association with the rest of the world, the greater the insularity of mind. The Englishman is somewhat affected by the size of his country; the Manxman still more, and the dwellers on the lighthouse rock most of all. Our homes are not physically isolated, save on scattered farms and ranches—where the worst results are found; but they are isolated in their interests and industries.

The thought used every day is thought about half a dozen people and their concerns, mainly their personal bodily care and comfort; the mental processes of the woman must needs be intensified in personality as they are limited in range. Hence her greater sensitiveness to all personal events, and that quick variation in attitude so inevitable in a mind whose daily work involves continual and instant change. *Varium et mutabile!* murmurs the man sagely—" A woman's privilege is to change her mind! " If the nature of his industry were such that he had to change his mind from cooking to cleaning, from cleaning to sewing, from sewing to nursing, from nursing to teaching, and so, backward, forward, crosswise and over again, from morning to night— he too would become adept in the lightning-change act.

The man adopts one business and follows it. He develops special ability, on long lines, in connection with wide interests—and so grows broader and steadier. The distinction is there, but it is not a distinction of sex. This is why the man forgets to mail the letter. He is used to one consecutive train of thought and action. She, used to a varying zigzag horde of little things, can readily accommodate a few more.

The home-bred brain of the woman continually puzzles and baffles the world-bred brain of the man; and from the beginning of their association it has an effect upon him. In childhood even he sees his sister serving in the home functions far more than he is required to do; she is taught to " clean up " where he is not; different values are assigned to the same act in boy or girl, and he is steadily influenced by it. The first effect of the home on the boy is seen very young in his contempt for girls, and girls' play or work. When, after a period of separation wherein he has consorted as far as possible only with boys and men, he is again drawn towards the girl on lines of sex-attraction, a barrier has risen between them which is never wholly removed.

He has immense areas of experience utterly unknown to her. His words and acts in a given case are modified by a thousand memories and knowledges which she has not; so word and act differ sharply, though the immediate exciting cause be the same. The very terms they use have different weight and meaning; the man must pick and choose and adopt a different speech in talking to a woman. He loves, he admires, he venerates; and from this attitude considering all her foolishness and ignorance as feminine and therefore charming, he is thus taught to worship ignoble things.

Charles Reade in his " Peg Woffington " describes that strong, brave, intelligent, and most charming woman as starting and screaming at a very distant rat—and her lover being therefore more strongly attracted to her.

[276]

HOME INFLUENCE ON MEN

Every sign of weakness, timidity, inability to understand and do, is deemed feminine and admired. Yet we all know that the best love is that which exalts, that which truly respects as well as fondly enjoys.

The smallness of the home-bound woman is not so injurious as the still smaller nature of the harem-bound, by as much as the home is larger and freer than the harem; but just as harem women limit man's growth, so do home women in slighter degree. The influence of women upon men is enormous. The home-bound mother limits the child and boy; the home-bound girl limits the youth; and the home-bound wife keeps up the pressure for life. It is not that women are really smaller-minded, weaker-minded, more timid and vacillating; but that whosoever, man or woman, lives always in a small dark place, is always guarded, protected, directed, and restrained, will become inevitably narrowed and weakened by it.

The woman is narrowed by the home and the man is narrowed by the woman. In proportion as man is great, as his interests are world-wide and his abilities high, is he injured by constant contact with a smaller mind. The more ordinary man feels it less, being himself nearer to the domestic plane of thought and action; but the belittling effect is there all the time.

THE HOME

If the boy's mother commanded as wide a range of action as his father; if her work were something to honour and emulate as well as her dear self something to love, the boy would never learn to use that bitter term "only mother." The father is a soldier, and the boy admires and longs to follow in great deeds. The father is a captain of industry—a skilled tradesman, a good physician—the boy has the father to love, and the work to admire as well. The father is something to other people, as well as all in all to him; and the boy has a new respect for him, seeing him in the social relation as well as the domestic. But his mother he sees only in the domestic relation and is early taught by the father himself, that he is "to take care of her!" Think of it! Teaching a child that he is to take care of his mother! A full-grown able-bodied woman will take a child of ten out with her at night—" to protect her!"

The exquisite absurdity of this position has no comparison or parallel. Think of a cow protected by a calf! A bear by a cub—a cat by a kitten! A tall, swift mare by a lanky colt! An alert, sharp-toothed collie by a tumbling, fat-pawed pup! How can a boy respect a thing that he, a child, can take care of! He can love, and does. He can take care of, and does He can later on support, and does; and even—this in a

recent instance of this sublime monstrosity—he can
" give away " *his own mother* in marriage ! No wonder
he so soon learns to say " only mother ! " When she is
not only mother, but mother and much besides, a real
human being, usefully exercising her human faculties,
the boy will make a better man.

Again, if his sister shared every freedom and advantage of childhood ; were equally educated, not only in
school, but in play, and in the ever-stimulating experi-
ences of daily life, he would feel far differently toward
her.

See two children on a journey, the mother holding
fast to the girl from beginning to end, only the car seat
and window for her ; the boy on the steps, the platform,
running about the station, asking questions of brakeman
and engineer, learning all the time. The boy gets five
times as much out of life as the girl, and he knows it.
It is not long before he is ashamed to play with girls,
and one cannot blame him.

Then comes the sweetheart. A new deep love, a great
overmastering reverence for the Woman, rises in his
heart. In the light of that love he accepts her as she is,
glorifying and idealising every weakness, every limitation, because it is hers. This is not well. He could
love her just as well, better, if his reverence were better

deserved, if the dignity of sex were enhanced by the dignity of a wise, strong, capable human being.

Of course the man feels that he would not love her as well if she were different. So he felt in past ages when she was even more feminine, even less human. So he will feel in coming ages, when she is truly his equal, a strong and understanding friend, a restful and stimulating companion, as well as the beautiful and loving woman. We have always been drawn together by love and always will be. The beautiful Georgian slave is beloved, the peasant lass, the princess; man loves woman, and she need not fear any change in that.

Our error lies in a false estimate of womanhood and manhood. The home, its labours, cares, and limitations we have called womanly; and everything else in life manly; wherefore if a woman manifested any power, ambition, interest, outside the home, that was un-womanly and must cost her her position as such. This is entirely wrong.

A woman is a woman and attractive to the men of her place and time, whether she be a beaded Hottentot, a rosy milkmaid, a pretty schoolma'am, or a veiled beauty of the Zenana.

We are taught that man most loves and admires the domestic type of woman. This is one of the roaring jokes of history. The breakers of hearts, the queens of romance, the goddesses of a thousand devotees, have not been cooks.

Women in general are attractive to men, but let a woman be glaringly conspicuous—the great singer, dancer, actress—immediately she has lovers without number. The best-loved women of all time have not been the little brown birds at home, by any means. Of course, when a man marries the queen of song he expects her to settle at once to the nest and remain there. But does he thereafter maintain the same degree of devotion that he bestowed before? It is not easy, after all, to maintain the height of romantic devotion for one's house-servant—or even one's housekeeper. The man loves his wife; but it is in spite of the home—not because of it. And wherever the shadow of unhappiness falls between them, wherever the sad record of sorrow and sin is begun, it is too often because love strays from that domestic area to follow a freer bird in a wider field.

It is not marriage which brings this danger, it is domestic service; it is not the perfect and mutual ownership of love, nor the sanction of law and religion; it is the one-sided ownership wherein the wife becomes the private servant, cook, cleaner, mender of rents, a valet, janitor, and chambermaid. Even as such she has more practical claim to respect than the wife who does not do this work nor any other; who is not the servant of the house, but merely its lady; who has absolutely no claim to human honour, no place in the social scheme, except that of the female.

Thus we find that the influence of the home upon man, as felt through the home-restricted woman, is not always for the best; and that even, as supposedly increasing the woman's charm, it does not work.

What follows further of the influence of the home upon man directly? How does it modify his personal life and development? The boy grows and breaks out of the home. It has for him a myriad ties—but he does not like to be tied. He strikes out for himself. If he is an English boy of the upper classes he is cut off early and sent to a boarding school; later he has " chambers " of his own. If an American, he simply goes into business, and in most cases away from home, boarding for a while. Then he loves, marries, and sets up a home of his own; a woman-and-child house, which he gladly and proudly maintains and in many ways enjoys.

So satisfied are we in our convictions regarding this status that we really and practically worship the home and family, holding it to be a man's first duty to maintain them. No man does it more patiently and generously than the American, and he is supported in his position by all the moral opinion of our world. He is " a good family man " we say, and can say no more. To stay at home evenings is especially desirable; the more of life that can be spent at home the better, we think, for all concrned. Now what is the real effect upon the man? Is the home, as we have it, satisfying to the real needs of man's nature; and if not, could it be improved?

The best proof of man's dissatisfaction with the home is found in his universal absence from it. It is not only that his work takes him out (and he sees to it that it does!) but the man who does not " have to work " also goes out, for pleasure.

The leisure classes in any country have no necessity upon them to leave home, yet their whole range of uneasy activity is to get outside, or to furnish constant diversion and entertainment, to while away the hours within. A human creature must work, play, or rest. Men work outside, play outside, and cannot rest more than so long at a time.

The man maintains a home, as part of his life-area, but does not himself find room in it. This is legitimate enough. It should be equally true of the woman. No human life of our period can find full exercise in a home.

Both need it, to rest in; to work from; but not to stay in.

This we find practically worked out in the average man's attitude toward the home. He provides it, cheerfully, affectionately, proudly; at any cost of labour, care, and ingenuity; but if he has to stay in it too much, he knows it softens and enfeebles him.

So he goes out, to meet men, to work and live as far as he can; and when he wants " a real good time,"—rest, recreation, healthful amusement,—he goes altogether with " the boys." The distant camp in the woods, the mountain climb, the hunting trip,—real rest and pleasure to the man are found with men away from home.

There is a sort of strain in the constant association with the smaller life, as there is in the painful keeping step with shorter legs; a slow, soft, gentle downward pull, against which every active man rebels. But he is bound to it, for life. The immutable laws of sex hold him to the woman; and as she is so he must be, more or less.

He is bound to the home by the needs of the child, and by the physical convenience and necessity of the place. If it were all that it should be, it would offer to the man rest, comfort, stimulus, and inspiration. In so far as it does, it is right. In so far as it does not, it is wrong. The ideal home shines clear and bright, at the end of the

day's work. Peace and happiness, relief from all effort
and anxiety, the calm replenishment of food and sleep,
the most delightful companionship. In some cases it
gives all this in fact. In many, many others the man
has to descend in coming home—to come down to it
instead of up. In it is a whole new field of cares,
worries, and labours. The primitive machinery of the
place, so imperfectly managed by the inexpert average
woman, jars rudely on his specialised consciousness.
The children are his pride and joy—that is as it should
be. But when their lack of intelligent care robs him of
his rest at night; and their lack of intelligent education,
makes them an anxiety and a distress instead of a comfort; that is as it should not be.

He does not bring his deficiencies in business home to
his wife and expect her to walk the floor at night with
them. The systematised man's work is done for the
day, and he comes home to shoulder a share of the
unsystematised inadequate woman's work. When the
woman of exceptional ability keeps the whole house
running smoothly, has no trouble with servants, no
trouble with the children, then the influence of the home
on man is pure beneficence. Such cases are most rare.
So used are we to the contrary, so besotted in our blind
adoration of ancient deficiencies, that we exhort the

young couple to face " the cares and troubles of married life " as if they really were an essential part of it. They have nothing to do with married life. They are the cares and troubles of our antiquated, mischievous system of housekeeping.

If men in their business were still using methods of a million years ago, they would need some exhortation too. It is marvellous that the same man who casts upon the scrap heap his most expensive machinery to replace it with still better, who constantly adjusts and readjusts his business to the latest demands of our rapidly changing time, can go home and contentedly endure the same petty difficulties which his father and his grandfather and all his receding ancestors endured in turn.

The inadequacy of the home, the gross imperfections of its methods and management have anything but a helpful influence on men. Necessary difficulties are to be borne or overcome, but to suffer with a sickle when a steam reaper is to be had is contemptible rather than elevating. There will be some pathetic protest here that it is a man's duty to help woman bear the troubles and difficulties of the home. The woman ardently believes this, and the man too, sometimes. Of all incredible impositions this is the most astounding.

Here we see half the human race, equally able with the

other half (equal does not mean similar, remember!), content to see every industry on earth taken away from them, save house-service and child-culture, growing up in the full knowledge and acceptance of this field of labour, generally declining to study said industries before undertaking them, cheerfully undertaking them without any pretense of efficiency, and then calling upon the other half of the world, upon men, who do everything else that is done to maintain our civilisation, to help them do their work!

We object to seeing the man harness the woman to the plough, and we are right. It is a poor way to work. A horse is more efficient, a steam-plough still better. It is time that we objected to the woman's effort to harness the man to the home, in all its cumbrous old-world inefficiencies. It is not more labour that the home wants, it is better machinery and administration.

Some hold that the feebleness of woman has a beneficent effect on man, draws out many of his nobler qualities. He should then marry a bed-ridden invalid—a purblind idiot—and draw them all out!

The essential weakness and deficiencies of the child are quite sufficient to call out all the strength and wisdom of both parents, without adding this travesty of childhood, this pretended helplessness of a full-grown woman.

[287]

THE HOME

The shame of it! That a mother, one who needs every attainable height of wisdom and power, should forego her own human development—to make good her claim on man for food and clothes and draw out his nobler qualities! The virtue of parentage is to be measured by its success, not by the amount of effort and sacrifice expended.

Granting that the care of the body is woman's especial work; the feeding, clothing, and cleaning of the world; she should by this time have developed some system of doing it which would make it less of a burden to the man as well as the woman. It is most discreditable to the business sense of a modern community that these vitally important life processes should be so clumsily performed, at such heavy cost of time, labour, and money.

The care and education of children are legitimately shared by the father. In this a man and his wife are truly partners. They engage in a common business and both labour in it. At present the man by no means does his share in this all-important work, save as he does it collectively, through school and college; there the woman is in default.

In the early years the man gives little thought and care to the child, this being supposed to be perfectly well attended to by the woman. That it is not, we may readily see; but the man can by no means assist in it; because he is so overburdened already in the material provision for the home.

The enormous and unnecessary expense of our domestic processes constitutes so excessive a drain on man's energy that it would be cruel, as well as useless, to expect him to do more.

With the reduction in expense which we have shown to be possible, lessening the cost of living by two-thirds and adding to productive labour by nearly half, the home, instead of being an unconscionable burden and ceaseless care, would become what it should be: an easily attained place of complete rest, comfort, peace, and invigoration.

The present influence of the home on men is felt most through this inordinate expense. The support of the family we have laid entirely upon man, thus developing in the dependent woman a limitless capacity for receiving things, and denying her the power to produce them. If this result remained in its simple first degree it would be bad enough; requiring of the man the maintenance of himself, a healthy able-bodied woman, and all the children, instead of having a vigorous helpmate, to honourably support herself, and do her share toward supporting her own children.

This result is cumulative, however. The confinement of the woman to the home, when she does not labour, results in her becoming a parasite, and the appetite of a parasite is insatiable. She has no sense of what we call " the value of money,"—meaning how much labour it represents,—because she never laboured for it. She received it from her father, all unthinking of where he got it, as is natural to a child ; and she continues to be a child, receiving as unthinkingly from her husband. This position we consider right, even beautiful ; man stoutly maintains it himself, and considers any effort of the woman to support herself as a reflection on him. He has arrogated to himself as a masculine function the power of producing wealth ; and considers it " unfeminine " for a woman to do it ; and as indicating a lack of manliness in him.

He should " consider the ant," in this capacity, or the bee ; and see that a purely masculine functionary has no other occupation whatsoever. He should consider also the male savage—he is " masculine " enough surely ; but he is little else. Last, nearest, and most practical he should consider the immense majority of women all over the world to-day who labour in the home. The Lady of the House is a pure parasite, almost wholly detrimental in her influence, but the Housewife is one of the hardest workers on earth. She works unceasingly; as Mrs. Diaz put it years ago, in a thoughtful husband's sudden consideration of his wife's working hours—" No noonings—no evenings—no rainy days!" She works harder and longer than the man, in a miscellaneous shifting field of effort far more exhausting to vitality than his specialised line; *and she bears children too!* If any man could make a boast equal to that of the mother of nine children—(whose son told me this himself) that she had never missed washing on Monday *but twice*—there might be some ground for the claim of superior strength.

In this kind of home—and it is still the rule on earth—what is the influence on man? Does this grade and amount of labour on the part of women lighten the burden, as we so fondly and proudly assume? It shows great ignorance of economic values to assume it.

The poorer a man is, the more he has to pay for everything. In this nine-tenths of our population where the woman works in the home, the man works harder and gets less comfort for his money than among those more successful men able to maintain a parasite. He sustains to the fullest degree all the economic disadvantages we have previously enumerated—the last extreme of wasteful purchase, the lowest stage of industrial exchange. With him, a self-supporting wife would at once double the family income, and the benefits of organised labour and purchase would reduce their expenses at the same time. The unnecessary expenses of a poor man's home are far greater in proportion than those of the rich man; and his enjoyment of the place is less.

He has always a tired wife, an unprogressive wife, a wife who cannot be to him what a strong, happy, growing woman should be. If she had eight hours (to take even the custom of our labour-wasting time) of specialised work, to be done with and left with eagerness for the beloved home, she would have a far fresher and more stimulating mind than she has after her ceaseless, confusing toils in the confined domestic atmosphere. The two, together, could afford a better house. The two, together, with twice the money and half the expense for food, could furnish their children with far better care than the overworked and undereducated housewife can give them.

The result upon the man would be pleasant, indeed. A clean, pretty, quiet home—not full of smell and steam and various messy industries, but simply a place to rest in when he comes to it. A wife as glad to be at home as he. Children also glad of the reunion hour, and the mother and father both delighted to be with their children. What is there in this a man should dread?

HOME INFLUENCE ON MEN

Would not such a home be good to come to, and would not its influence be wholly pleasant? Our Puritanism shrinks at the idea of homes being wholly pleasant. They should be something of a trial, we think, for our soul's good. The wife and mother ought to be tired and overworked, careworn, dirty, anxious from hour to hour as she tries to " mind the children " and all her other trades as well. The man ought to be contented with the exhausted wife, the screaming babies, the ill-cooked food, the general weary chaos of the place, the endless demand on his single purse.

Is he? What is the average workingman's attitude toward this supposed haven of rest? The statistics of the temperance society are enough to show us the facts. A man does not like that kind of a place—and why should he?

He is tired, working for six or ten; and to go from his completed labour of the day, back to his wife's un-completed labour of the day and night, does not rest him. He wants companionship. She cannot give it him. Her talk is of the suds, the coal, the need of shoes, clothes, furniture, utensils—everything!

He wants amusement, she cannot give it him. An exhausted woman, taken every day, is not entertaining. The children are, or should be, in bed. The wife wants

[293]

rest and companionship, and amusement, too; but that is another story. We are considering the man. She must stay at home in any case, the home being her place; but he does not have to, and out he goes.

The instinctive demands of a highly developed human creature, a social creature, are strong within him; needs as vital as the needs of the body, and utterly unsatisfied at home. Out he goes, and to the one pleasant open door—the saloon. Ease, freedom, comfort, pleasant company, talk of something new, amusement—these are the main needs; and if a stimulating drink is the necessary price, there is nothing in the average man's ill-fed stomach, overdeveloped personal selfishness, or untrained conscience, to refuse it.

The measureless results in evil we all know well. Many are the noble souls devoting their life's efforts to the closing of the saloon, the driving back of erring man to the safe and supposedly all-satisfying shelter of the home. We do not dream that it is the home which drives him there.

One thing we have divined at last; that insufficient and ill-chosen food, villainously cooked, is one great cause of man's need for stimulants. Under this much illumination we now strive mightily to make man's private cook a better cook. If every man's wife were a

Delmonico, if his appetites were catered to with absolute skill and ingenuity, would that teach him temperance and self-control?

The worse the private cook, the greater the physical need for stimulant. The better the private cook, the greater the self-indulgence developed in the happy Epicurean. But good or bad, no man of any grade can get the social stimulus he needs by spending every evening with his cook!

That is the key to the whole thing. Your cook may be "a treasure," she may cater to your needs most exquisitely, she may also be the mother of your children, as has been the case from the earliest times; but she is none the less your own personal servant, and as such not your social equal. You may love her dearly and honour her in her female capacity, also honour the excellence of her cooking, but you are not satisfied with her conversation or her skill in games.

The influence of the home with a working wife is not all that could be desired; and we may turn with some hope of better things to the home with a parasite wife. Here certainly the man comes home to rest and peace and comfort, and to satisfying companionship with the "eternal feminine." Here is a woman who is nothing on earth but a woman, not even a cook. Here, of course, the food is satisfactory; the children all a father's heart could wish, having the advantage of the incessant devotion of an entire mother; the machinery of the home, so painfully prominent to the workingman, is here running smoothly and unseen; and the whole thing is well within the means of the proud " provider."

What the food supply is in the hands of the housemaid we have seen. What the child is in the hands of the nursemaid, we may see anywhere. The parasitic woman by no means uses the time free of housework to devote herself to her children. A mother is essentially a worker. When a woman does not work it dries the very springs of motherhood. The idler she is, the less she does for her children. The rich man's children are as often an anxiety and disappointment to him as the poor man's.

The expense of the place is a thing of progressive dimensions. The home of the parasitic woman is a bottomless pit for money. She is never content. How could a human creature be content in such an unnatural position? She is supplied with nourishment; she has such social stimulus as her superficial contact with her kind affords, but nothing comes out; there is no commensurate action.

In the uneasy distress of this position her only idea of relief is to get something more; if she is not satisfied after one dinner, get or give another dinner; if not satisfied with one dress, get two, get twenty, get them all! If the home does not satisfy, by all means get another one in the country; perhaps that will feel different; try first one and then the other. If the two, or three, should pall, get a yacht, go to some other country, get more things to put in the home or on one's pretty body; get, get, get! and never a thought of the ease and freedom and joy that would come of Doing. Not of playing at doing, with a hot poker or a modelling tool—but really doing human work. It does not occur to her, and it does not occur to him. He thinks it right and beautiful to maintain the dainty domestic vampire, and pours forth his life's service to meet her insatiate demands. All the reward he asks is her love and faith, her sweet companionship.

May we look, then, in homes of this class for an ideal influence on man? Consecrating his life to the business of not only feeding and clothing, but profusely decorating and amusing a useless woman,—does this have an elevating effect on him? When he thinks of how charming she will look in the costly fur, the lace, the jewels, how she will enjoy the new home, the new carriage, the new furniture; of her fresh and ceaseless delight in her " social functions "—does his heart leap within him?

THE HOME

He performs wonders in business, honest or dishonest, useful to mankind or cruel; he slowly relinquishes the ideals of his youth, devotes his talents to whatever will make the most money, even prostitutes his political conscience, and robs the city and the state, in order to meet the demands of that fair, plump, smiling Queen of the Home.

And she gives in return—? Her influence is—? The working wife does not lift a man up very high. The parasite wife pulls him down. The home of the working wife gives to boy and man the impression that women are servants. The home of the idle wife gives to boy and man the impression that women are useless and rapacious; but, we must have them because they are women.

This is the worst that the home shows us, and is, fortunately, confined to a minority of cases. But it is none the less an evil influence of large extent. It leaves to the woman no functions whatever save those of the female, and, as exaggeration is never health, does not improve her as a female.

The really restful and stimulating companionship of man and wife, the general elevating social intercourse between men and women, is not to be found in the homes of the wealthy any more than in those of the poor. The demands upon the man are unending, and the returns in good to body or mind bear no proportion to the expense. The woman who has no other field of usefulness or growth than a home wherein she is not even the capable servant, cannot be the strong, noble, uplifting creature who does good to man; but rapidly becomes the type most steadily degrading.

XV

HOME AND SOCIAL PROGRESS

IF there is one fact more patent than another in regard to social evolution, it is that our gain is far greater in material progress than in personal. The vast and rapid increase in wealth, in power, in knowledge, in facility and speed in production and distribution; the great spread of political, religious, and educational advantages; all this is in no way equalled by any gain in personal health and personal happiness.

The world grows apace; the people do not keep pace with it. Our most important machines miss much of their usefulness because the brain of the workman has not improved as rapidly as the machine. Great systems of transportation, involving intricate mechanical arrangement, break continually at this, their weakest link —the human being. We create and maintain elaborate systems of justice and equity, of legislation, administration, education; and they are always open to failure in this same spot—the men are not equal to the system.

The advance in public good is far greater than the advance in private good. We have improved every facility in living; but we still live largely as before—sick, feeble, foolishly quarrelling over small personal matters, unaware of our own great place in social evolution. This has always been known to us and has been used only to prove our ancient theory as to the corrupt and paltry stuff humanity is made of. " Frail creatures of dust, and feeble as frail," is our grovelling confession; and to those who try to take comfort in our undeniable historic gains, it has been triumphantly pointed out that, gain as we would, " the human heart " was no better—" poor human nature " was unimprovable. This is utterly untrue.

Human nature has changed and improved in tremendous ratio; and, if its improvement has been strangely irregular, far greater in social life than in personal life, it is for a very simple reason. All these large social processes which show such marked improvement are those wherein people work together in legitimate specialised lines in the world. These personal processes which have not so improved, the parts of life which are still so limited and imperfectly developed, may be fully accounted for by their environment—the ancient and unchanging home. Bring the home abreast of our other institutions; and our personal health and happiness will equal our public gains.

THE HOME

Once more it must be stated that the true home, the legitimate and necessary home, the home in right proportion and development, is wholly good. It is at once the beautiful beginning, the constant help, and one legitimate end of a life's work. To the personal life, the physical life, this is enough. To the social life, it is not. If human duty had no other scope than to maintain and reproduce this species of animal, that duty might be accomplished in the home. The purely maternal female, having no other reason for being than to bear and rear young; a marauding male, to whom the world was but a hunting ground wherein to find food for his family—these, and their unimproved successors, need nothing more than homes. But human duty is not so limited. These processes of reproduction are indeed essential to our human life, as are the processes of respiration and digestion, but they do not constitute that life, much less conclude it.

As human beings, our main field of duty lies in promoting social advance. To maintain ourselves and our families is an animal duty we share with the other animals; to maintain each other, and, by so doing to increase our social efficiency, is human duty, first, last, and always. We have always seen the necessity for social groups, religious, political, and other; we have more or less fulfilled our social functions therein; but we have in the main supposed that all this common effort was merely for the greater safety and happiness of homes; and when the interests of the home and those of the state clashed, most of us have put home first.

The first person to learn better was that very earliest of social servants, the soldier. He learned first of all to combine for the common good, and though his plane of service was the lowest of all, mere destruction, the group sentiments involved were of the highest order. The destructive belligerence of the male, and his antecedent centuries of brute combat, made fighting qualities most prominent; but the union and organisation required for successful human warfare called out high social qualities, too. The habit of acting together necessarily develops in the brain the power and desire to act together; the fact that success or failure, life or death, advantage or injury, depends on collective action, necessarily develops the social consciousness. This modification we find in the army everywhere, gradually increasing with race-heredity; and, long since, so far overwhelming the original egoism of the individual animal, that the common soldier habitually sacrifices his life to the public service without hesitation.

The steps in social evolution must always be made in

this same natural order, from one stage of development to another, by means of existing qualities. Primitive man had no altruism, he had no honour, his courage was flickering and wholly personal; he had no sense of order and discipline, of self-control and self-sacrifice; but he had a strong inclination to fight, and by means of that one tendency he was led into relations which developed all those other qualities.

It is easy to see that this stage of our social development was diametrically opposed by the home. The interests of the home demanded personal service; the habits of the home bred industry and patience; the influence of the inmates of the home, of the women and children, did not promote martial qualities. So our valorous ancestor promptly left home and went a-fighting, for thousands and thousands of years, while human life was maintained by the women at home.

When men gradually learned to apply their energies to production, instead of destruction; learning in slow, painful, costly ages that wealth was in no way increased by robbing, nor productive strength by slaughter; they were able to apply to their new occupations some of the advantageous qualities gained in the old. Thus industry grew, spread, organised, and the power and riches and wisdom of the world began to develop.

HOME AND SOCIAL PROGRESS

As far back as history can go we find some men producing, even while a large and important caste was still fighting. The warriors sought wealth by plundering other nations, not realising that if the other nations had been all warriors there would have been nothing to plunder. Slowly the wealth-makers overtook the wealth-takers, caught up with them, passed them; and now the greater part of the masculine energy of the world is devoted to productive industry in some form, and the army is recruited from the lowest ranks of life.

In this new field of social service, productive industry, what is the influence of the home? At first it was altogether good. To wean the man from his all too-natural instinct to wander, kill, and rob, the attractions of home life were needed. To centre and localise his pride and power, to make him bend his irregular expansive tendencies to the daily performance of labour, was a difficult task; and here again he had to be led by the force of existing qualities. The woman was the great drawing power here, the ease and comfort of the place, the growing love of family, and these influences slowly overcame the warrior and bound him to the plough.

Thus far the home influence led him up, and, in turn, his military qualities lifted the home industries from the feminine plane to the human. To produce wealth for the home to consume was a better position than that of living by plunder; but we should have small cause to glory in the march of civilisation if that was all we had done.

Just as the fierce and brutal savage, entering into military combination, under no better instincts than self-defence and natural belligerence, yet learned by virtue of that combination new and noble qualties; so the still fierce and brutal soldier, entering into industrial combination under no better instincts than those of sex-attraction and physical wants in increasing degree, yet learned, by virtue of this form of union, new qualities even more valuable to the race.

The life of any society is based on the successful inter-action of its members, rather than the number of its families. For instance, in those vast, fat, ancient empires, where a vast population, scattered over wide territory, supported local life in detached families, by individual effort; there was almost no national life, no general sense of unity, no conscious connection of interests. The one tie was taxation; and if some passing conqueror annexed a province, the only change was in the tax-collector, and the people were not injured unless he demanded more than the previous one.

A vital nation must exist in the vivid common consciousness of its people; a consciousness naturally developed by enlarging social functions, by undeniable common interests and mutual services. If any passing conqueror were to annex—or seek to annex—a portion of our vast territory, he would find no slice of jellyfish, no mere cellular existence with almost no organised life. He would find that every last and least part of the country was vitally one with the whole, and would submit to no dismemberment. This social consciousness, on which our civilised life depends, in the growth of which lies social progress, is not developed in the home. On the contrary it is opposed by it. Up to a certain level the home promotes social development. Beyond that level it hinders it, if allowed to do so.

Self-interest drove men into military combination—where they learned much. Family interest drove them into industrial activity, and even allowed a low form of combination. But social interest is what leads us all farthest and highest; the impulse to live, not for self-preservation only, not for reproduction only, but for social progress. It should not be hard to see that these apparently dissimilar and opposed interests can only be harmonised by the dominance of the greatest. The man who would strive for his own advantage at the expense of his family, we call a brute. The man who strives for the advantage of his family at the expense of his country—we should call a traitor! Yet this is the common attitude of the citizen of to-day, and in this attitude he is maintained and extolled by the home! The soldier who would seek to save his own life to the injury of the army we promptly shoot. If he should seek to save his home at the same risk, we should still dishonour and punish him.

The army, very highly developed in a very low scheme of action, knows that neither self nor family must stand for a moment against the public service. Industry is not so well organised as warfare, and so our scale of industrial virtues is not so high. We degrade and punish for " conduct unbecoming an officer and a gentleman " ; but we take no cognisance of " conduct unbecoming a manufacturer and a gentleman," unless he is an open malefactor. Yet a manufacturer is a far higher and more valuable social servant than a soldier of any grade. We do not yet know the true order of importance in our social functions, nor their distinctly organic nature.

With our proven capacity, why do we manifest so little progress in industrial organisation and devotion? A student of prehuman evolution, one familiar only with nature's long, slow, stumbling process of developing by exclusion—like driving a flock of sheep by killing those who went the wrong way—might answer the question in this manner: That we have not been engaged in industrial processes long enough to develop the desired qualities. This is usually considered the evolutionary standpoint; and from it we are advised not to be impatient, and are told that a few thousand years' more killing will do much for us.

But social evolution takes place on quite other grounds. We have added education to heredity; mutual help to the cruel and wasteful processes of elimination. The very essence of social relation is its transmission of individual advance to the collective. Physical evolution acts only through physical heredity; we have that in common with all animals; but we have also social heredity, that great psychic current of transmitted wisdom and emotion which immortalises the gains of the past and generalises the gains of the present.

A system of free public education does more to develop the brains of a people than many thousand years of " natural selection," and does not prevent natural selection, either,

The one capacity wherein the world does not progress as it should is the power of social intelligence; of a ra-

[309]

tional, efficiently acting, common consciousness. Our " body politic " is like that of a vigorous, well-grown idiot. We have all the machinery for large, rich, satisfying life; and inside is the dim, limited mind, incapable of enjoyment or action. It has been found in recent years that idiocy may result from a too small skull; the bones have not enlarged, and the brain, compressed and stunted, cannot perform its functions. In one case this was most cruelly proven, by an operation upon an old man, from birth and idiot. His skull was opened and so treated as to give more room to the imprisoned brain, and, with what hopeless horror can be imagined, the man became intelligently conscious at last—conscious of what his life had been!

There is some similar arrest in the development of the social consciousness; else our cities would not sit gnawing and tearing at themselves, indifferent to dirt, disease, or vice, and enjoying only physical comfort. If any operation should give sudden new light to this long-clouded civic brain, we might feel the same horror of the years behind us, but not the same hopelessness—society is immortal.

It is here suggested that one check to the social development proper to our time is the pressure of the rudimentary home. We are quite willing to admit that a home life we consider wrong, as the Chinese or Turkish, can paralyse a nation. We have even come to see that the position of women is a good gauge of progress. Is it so hard, then, to admit at least a possibility that the position of our women, the nature of our homes, may have some important influence upon our social growth? There is no demand that we destroy the home, any more than that we destroy the women, *but we must change their relative position.*

The brain is the medium of social contact, the plane of human development. The savage is incapable of large relation because his mental area is not big enough; he is not used to such extensive combinations. Where the brain is accustomed only to incessant consideration of its own private interests, and to direct personal service of those interests, it is thereby prevented from developing the capacity for seeing the public interests, and for indirect collective service of those interests. The habit, continuous and unrelieved, of thinking in a small circuit checks the power to think in a large circuit.

This arrested brain development, this savage limitation to the personal, and mainly to the physical, is what we have so rigidly enforced upon women. The primitive home to the primitive mind is sufficient; but the progress of the mind requires a commensurate progress of the home—and has not had it. Owing to our peculiar and unnatural division of life-area, half the race has been free to move on, and so has accomplished much for all of us; but the other half, being confined to the same position it occupied in the infancy of society, has been denied that freedom and that progress. Owing again to the inexorable reunion of these divided halves in each child, physical heredity does what it can to bridge the gulf, the ever-widening gulf; pouring into the stationary woman some share of the modern abilities of social man; and also forcing upon the moving man some share of the primitive disabilities of the domestic woman. We thus have a strange and painful condition of life.

Social progress, attained wholly by the male, gives to the unprogressive woman unrest, discontent, disease. The more society advances, the less she can endure her ancient restrictions. Hence arises much evil and more unhappiness. Domestic inertia, maintained by the woman, gives to the progressive man a tremendous undertow of private selfishness and short-sightedness. Hence more evil, far more; for the social processes are the most important; and a deeper unhappiness too; for the shame of the social traitor, the helplessness of the home-bound man who knows his larger duty but cannot meet it, is a higher plane of suffering than hers, and also adds to hers continually.

All this evil and distress is due not at all to the blessed influence of the true home, suited to our time, but to the anything but blessed influence of a home suited to the Stone Age—or perhaps the Bronze! It is not in the least necessary. The change we require does not involve the loss of one essential good and lovely thing. It does not injure womanhood, but improves it. It does not injure childhood, but improves it. It does not injure manhood, but improves that too.

What is the proposed change? It is the recognition of a new order of duties, a new scale of virtues; or rather it is the practical adoption of that order long since established by the facts of business, the science of government, and by all great religions. Our own religion in especial, the most progressive, the most social, gives no sanction whatever to our own archaic cult of home-worship.

What is there in the teachings of Christianity to justify—much less command—this devotion to animal comfort, to physical relations, to the A B C of life? In his own life Christ rose above all family ties; his disciples he called to leave all and follow him; the devotion he recognised was that of Mary to the truth, not of Martha to the housekeeping; and the love he taught, that love which is the beginning and the end of Christian life, is not the love of one's own merely, but of the whole world. " Whoso careth not for his own is worse than an infidel " —truly. And whoso careth only for his own is *no better!*

Besides—and this should reconcile the reluctant heart —this antiquated method of serving the family *does not serve them to the best advantage.* In what way does a man best benefit his family? By staying at home and doing what he can with his own two hands—whereby no family on earth would ever have more than the labour of one affectionate amateur could provide; or by going out from the home and serving other people in a specialised trade—whereby his family and all families are gradually supplied with peace and plenty, supported and protected by the allied forces of civilisation?

In what way does a woman best benefit her family? By staying at home and doing what she can with her own two hands—whereby no family ever has more than the labour of one affectionate amateur can provide—or by enlarging her motherhood as man has enlarged his fatherhood, and giving to her family the same immense advantages that he has given it? We have always assumed that the woman could do most by staying at home.

Is this so? Can we prove it? Why is that which is so palpably false of a man held to be true of a woman? " Because men and woman are different! " will be stoutly replied. Of course they are different—in sex, *but not in humanity*. In every human quality and power they are alike; and the right service of the home, the right care and training of the child, call for human qualities and powers, not merely for sex-distinctions.

The home, in its arbitrary position of arrested development, does not properly fulfil its own essential functions—much less promote the social ones. Among the splendid activities of our age it lingers on, inert and blind, like a clam in a horse-race.

It hinders, by keeping woman a social idiot, by keeping the modern child under the tutelage of the primeval mother, by keeping the social conscience of the man crippled and stultified in the clinging grip of the domestic conscience of the woman. It hinders by its enormous expense; making the physical details of daily life a heavy burden to mankind; whereas, in our stage of civilisation, they should have been long since reduced to a minor incident.

Consider what the mere protection and defence of life used to cost, when every man had to be fighter most of his life. Ninety per cent., say, of masculine energy went to defend life; while the remaining ten, and the women, in a narrow, feeble way, maintained it. They lived, to be sure, fighting all the time for the sorry privilege. Now we have systematised military service so that only a tiny fraction of our men, for a very short period of life, need be soldiers; and peace is secured, not by constant painful struggles, but by an advanced economic system. " Eternal vigilance " may be " the price of liberty," but it is a very high price; and paid only by the barbarian who has not risen to the stage of civilised service.

Organisation among men has reduced this wasteful and crippling habit of being every-man-his-own-soldier. We do not have to carry a rifle and peer around every street-corner for a hidden foe. As a result the released energy of the ninety per cent. men, a tenth being large allowance for all the fighting necessary, is now poured into the channels that lead to wealth, peace, education, general progress.

Yet we are still willing that the personal care of life, the service of daily physical needs, shall monopolise as many women as that old custom of universal warfare monopolised men! Ninety per cent. of the feminine energy of the world is still spent in ministering laboriously to the last details of bodily maintenance; and the other tenth is supposed to do nothing but supervise the same tasks, and flutter about in fruitless social amusement. This crude waste of half the world's force keeps back human progress just as heavily as the waste of the other half did.

By as much as the world has grown toward peace and power and unity since men left off spending their lives in universal warfare, will it grow further toward that much-desired plane when women leave off spending their lives in universal house-service. The mere release of that vast fund of energy will in itself increase all the facilities of living; but there is a much more important consequence.

The omnipresent domestic ideal is a deadly hinderance to the social ideal. When half our population honestly believe that they have no duties outside the home, the other half will not become phenomenal statesmen. This cook-and-housemaid level of popular thought is the great check. The social perspective is entirely lost; and a million short-sighted homes, each seeing only its own interests, cannot singly or together grasp the common good which would benefit them all.

That the home has improved as much as it has is due to the freedom of man outside it. That it is still so clumsy, so inadequate, so wickedly wasteful of time, of money, of human life, is due to the confinement of woman inside it.

What sort of citizens do we need for the best city—the best state—the best country—the best world? We need men and women who are sufficiently large-minded to see and feel a common need, to work for a common good, to rejoice in the advance of all, and to know as the merest platitude that their private advantage is to be assured *only* by the common weal. That kind of mind is not bred in the kitchen.

A citizenship wherein all men were either house-servants or idlers would not show much advance. Neither does a community wherein all women, save that noble and rapidly increasing minority of self-supporting ones, are either house-servants or idlers. Our progress rests on the advance of the people, all the people; the development of an ever-widening range of feeling, thought, action; while its flowers are found in all the higher arts and sciences, it is rooted firmly in economic law.

This little ganglion of aborted economic processes, the home, tends to a sort of social paralysis. In its innumerable little centres of egoism and familism are sunk and lost the larger vibrations of social energy which should stimulate the entire mass. Again, society's advance rests on the personal health, sanity, and happiness of its members. The home, whose one justification is in its ministering to these, does not properly fulfil its purpose, and cannot unless it is managed on modern lines.

Social progress rests on the smooth development of personal character, the happy fulfilment of special function. The home, in its ceaseless and inexorable demands, stops this great process of specialisation in women, and checks it cruelly in men. A man's best service to society lies in his conscientious performance of the work he is best fitted for. But the service of the home demands that he do the work he is best paid for. Man after man, under this benumbing, strangling pressure, is diverted from his true path in social service, and condemned to " imprisonment with hard labour for life."

The young man, for a time, is comparatively free; and looks forward eagerly to such and such a line of growth and large usefulness. But let him marry and start a home, and he must do, not what he would—what is best for him and best for all of us; but what he must— what he can be sure of pay for. We have always supposed this to be a good thing, as it forced men to be industrious. As if it was any benefit to society to have men industrious in wrong ways—or useless ways, or even slow, stupid, old-fashioned ways!

THE HOME

Human advance calls for each man's best, for his special faculties, for the work he loves best and can therefore do best and do most of. This work is not always the kind that commands the greater wages; at least the immediate wages he must have. The market will pay best for what it wants, and what it wants is almost always what it is used to, and often what is deadly bad for it. Having a family to support, in the most wasteful possible way, multiplies a man's desire for money; but in no way multiplies his ability, his social value.

Therefore the world is full of struggling men, putting in for one and trying to take out for ten; and in this struggle seeking continually for new ways to cater to the tastes of the multitude, and especially to those of the rich; that they may obtain the wherewithal to support the ten, or six, or simply the one; who though she be but one and not a worker, is quite ready to consume more than any ten together! Social advantage is ruthlessly sacrificed to private advantage in our life to-day; not to necessary and legitimate private interests either; not to the best service of the individual, but to false and scandalously wasteful private interests; to the maintenance and perpetuation of inferior people.

The position is this: the home, as now existing, costs three times what is necessary to meet the same needs. It

involves the further waste of nearly half the world's
labour. It does not fulfil its functions to the best advantage, thus robbing us again. It maintains a low
grade of womanhood, overworked or lazy; it checks the
social development of men as well as women, and, most of
all, of children. The man, in order to meet this unnecessary expense, must cater to the existing market; and
the existing market is mainly this same home, with its
crude tastes and limitless appetites. Thus the man, to
maintain his own woman in idleness, or low-grade labour,
must work three times as hard as is needful, to meet the
demands of similar women; the home-bound woman
clogging the whole world.

Change this order. Set the woman on her own feet,
as a free, intelligent, able human being, quite capable of
putting into the world more than she takes out, of being
a producer as well as a consumer. Put these poor antiquated " domestic industries " into the archives of past
history; and let efficient modern industries take their
place, doing far more work, far better work, far cheaper
work in their stead.

With an enlightened system of feeding the world we
shall have better health—and wiser appetites. The
more intelligent and broad-minded woman will assuredly
promote a more reasonable, healthful, beautiful, and

economical system of clothing, for her own body and that of the child. The wiser and more progressive mother will at last recognise child-culture as an art and science quite beyond the range of instinct, and provide for the child such surroundings, such training, as shall allow of a rapid and enormous advance in human character.

The man, relieved of two-thirds of his expenses; provided with double supplies; properly fed and more comfortable at home than he ever dreamed of being, and associated with a strong, free, stimulating companion all through life, will be able to work to far better purpose in the social service, and with far greater power, pride, and enjoyment.

The man and woman together, both relieved of most of their personal cares, will be better able to appreciate large social needs and to meet them. Each generation of children, better born, better reared, growing to their full capacity in all lines, will pour into the world a rising flood of happiness and power. Then we shall see social progress.

XVI

LINES OF ADVANCE

IT will be helpful and encouraging for us to examine the development of the home to this date, and its further tendencies; that we may cease to regret here, and learn to admire there; that we may use our personal powers definitely to resist the undertow of habit and prejudice, and definitely to promote all legitimate progress.

There is a hopelessness in the first realisation of this old-world obstacle still stationary in our swift to-day; but there need not be. While apparently as strong as ever, it has in reality been undermined on every side by the currents of evolution; its whilom prisoners have been stimulated and strengthened by the unavoidable force of those same great currents, and little remains to do beyond the final opening of one's own eyes to the facts— not one's grandmother's eyes, but one's *own*—and the beautiful work of reconstruction.

Examine the main root of the whole thing—the exclusive confinement of women to the home, to their feminine functions and a few crude industries; and see

[323]

how rapidly that condition is changing. The advance of women, during the last hundred years or so, is a phenomenon unparalleled in history. Never before has so large a class made as much progress in so small a time. From the harem to the forum is a long step, but she has taken it. From the ignorant housewife to the president of a college is a long step, but she has taken it. From the penniless dependent to the wholly self-supporting and often other-supporting business woman, is a long step, but she has taken it. She who knew so little is now the teacher; she who could do so little is now the efficient and varied producer; she who cared only for her own flesh and blood is now active in all wide good works around the world. She who was confined to the house now travels freely, the foolish has become wise, and the timid brave. Even full political equality is won in more than one country and state; it is a revolution of incredible extent and importance, and its results are already splendidly apparent.

This vast number of human beings, formerly as separate as sand grains and as antagonistic as the nature of their position compelled, are now organising, from house to club, from local to general, in federations of city, state, nation, and world. The amount of social energy accumulated by half of us is no longer possible of confinement to that half; the woman has inherited her share, and has grown so large and strong that her previous surroundings can no longer contain or content her.

The socialising of this hitherto subsocial, wholly domestic class, is a marked and marvellous event, now taking place with astonishing rapidity. That most people have not observed it proves nothing. Mankind has never yet properly perceived historic events until time gave him the perspective his narrow present horizon denied.

Where most of our minds are home-enclosed, like the visual range of one sitting in a hogshead, general events make no impression save as they impinge directly on that personal area. The change in the position of woman, largely taking place in the home, is lost to general view; and so far as it takes place in public, is only perceived in fractions by most of us.

To man it was of course an unnatural and undesired change; he did not want it, did not see the need or good of it, and has done all he could to prevent it. To the still inert majority of women, content in their position, or attributing their growing discontent to other causes, it is also an unnatural and undesired change. Ideas do not change as fast as facts, with most of us. Mankind

[325]

in general, men and women, still believe in the old established order, in woman's ordination to the service of bodily needs of all sorts; in the full sufficiency of maternal instinct as compared with any trivial propositions of knowledge and experience; in the noble devotion of the man who spends all his labours to furnish a useless woman with luxuries, and all the allied throng of ancient myths and falsehoods.

Thus we have not been commonly alive to the full proportions of the woman's movement, or its value. The facts are there, however. Patient Griselda has gone out, or is going, faster and faster. The girls of to-day, in any grade of society, are pushing out to do things instead of being content to merely eat things, wear things, and dust things. The honourable instinct of self-support is taking the place of the puerile acceptance of gifts, and beyond self-support comes the still nobler impulse to give to others; not corrupting charity, but the one all-good service of a life's best work. Measuring the position of woman as it has been for all the years behind us up to a century or so ago with what it is to-day, the distance covered and the ratio of progress is incredible. It rolls up continually, accumulatively; and another fifty years will show more advance than the past five hundred.

LINES OF ADVANCE

This alone is enough to guarantee the development of the home. No unchanging shell can contain a growing body, something must break; and the positive force of growth is stronger than the negative force of mere adhesion of particles. A stronger, wiser, nobler woman must make a better home.

In the place itself, its customs and traditions, we can also note great progress. The " domestic industries " have shrunk and dwindled almost out of sight, so greedily has society sucked at them and forced them out where they belong.

The increasing difficulties which assail the housekeeper, either in trying to occupy the primeval position of doing her own work, or in persuading anyone else to do it for her, are simply forcing us, however reluctantly, to the adoption of better methods. Even in the most neglected field of all, the care and education of the little child, some progress has been made. Education in the hands of men, broad-minded, humanly loving men, has crept nearer and nearer to the cradle; and now even women, and not only single women, but *even mothers,* are beginning to study the nature and needs of the child. The more they study, the more they learn, the more impossible become the home conditions. The mother cannot herself alone do all that is necessary for her children, to say nothing of continuing to be a companion to her husband, a member of society, and a still growing individual.

She can sacrifice herself in the attempt,—often does,—but the child has a righteous indifference to such futile waste of life. He does not require a nervous, exhausted, ever-present care, and it is by no means good for him. He wants a strong, serene, lovely mother for a comfort, a resource, an ideal; but he also wants the care of a trained highly qualified teacher, and the amateur mama cannot give it to him. Motherhood is a common possession of every female creature; a joy, a pride, a nobly useful function. Teacherhood is a profession, a specialised social function, no more common to mothers than to fathers, maids, or bachelors. The ceaseless, anxious strain to do what only an experienced nurse and teacher can do, is an injury to the real uses of motherhood.

Why do we dread having children, as many of our much-extolled mothers so keenly do? Partly the physical risk and suffering, which are not necessary to a normal woman,—and more the ensuing care, labour, and anxiety,—and oh,—" the responsibility!" The more modern the mother is, the more fit for a higher plane of execution, the more unfit she is for the lower plane, the old primitive plane of home-teaching.

If your father is a combination of all college professors you may get part of a college training at home—but not the best part. If your mother is a born teacher, a trained teacher, an experienced teacher, you may get part of your schooling at home—but not the best part. There would never have been a school or college on earth, if every man had remained content with teaching his boys at home. There will never be any proper standard of training for little children while each woman remains content with caring for her own at home. But the housewife is changing. These ways no longer satisfy her. She insists on more modern methods, even in her ancient labours.

Then follows the equally different attitude of the housemaid; her rebellion, refusal, retirement from the field; and the immense increase in mechanical convenience seeping in steadily from outside, and doing more to " undermine the home " than any wildest exhortations of reformers. The gas range, the neat and perfect utensils, these have in themselves an educational reaction; we cannot now maintain the atmosphere " where greasy Joan doth keel the pot." The pot is a white enamelled double boiler, and Joan need not be greasy save of *malice prepense.* Besides the improvement of utensils, we have in our cities and in most of the smaller towns that insidious new system of common supply of domestic necessities, which webs together the once so separate homes by a network of pipes and wires.

Our houses are threaded like beads on a string, tied, knotted, woven together, and in the cities even built together; one solid house from block-end to block-end; their boasted individuality maintained by a thin partition wall. The tenement, flat, and apartment house still further group and connect us; and our claim of domestic isolation becomes merely another domestic myth. Water is a household necessity and was once supplied by household labour, the women going to the wells to fetch it. Water is now supplied by the municipality, and flows among our many homes as one. Light is equally in common; we do not have to make it for ourselves.

Where water and light are thus fully socialised, why are we so shy of any similar progress in the supply of food? Food is no more a necessity than water. If we are willing to receive our water from an extra-domestic pipe—why not our food? The one being a simple element and the other a very complex combination makes a difference, of course; but even so we may mark great progress. Some foods, more or less specific, and of universal use, were early segregated, and the making of them became a trade, as in breadstuffs, cheese, and confectionery. Where this has been done we find great progress, and an even standard of excellence. In America, where the average standard of bread-making is very low, we regard " baker's bread " as a synonym for inferiority; but even here, if we consider the saleratus bread of the great middle west, and all the sour, heavy, uncertain productions of a million homes, the baker bears comparison with the domestic cook. It is the maintenance of the latter that keeps the former down; where the baker is the general dependence he makes better bread.

Our American baker's bread has risen greatly in excellence as we make less and less at home. All the initial processes of the food supply have been professionalised. Our housewife does not go out crying, " Dilly-dilly! Dilly-dilly! You must come and be killed "—and then wring the poor duck's neck, pick and pluck it with her own hands; nor does the modern father himself slay the fatted calf—all this is done as a business. In recent years every article of food which will keep, every article which is in common demand, is prepared as a business.

The home-blinded toiler has never climbed out of her hogshead to watch this rising tide, but it is nearly up to the rim, ready to pour in and float her out. Every delicate confection, every pickle, sauce, preserve, every species of biscuit and wafer, and all sublimated and differentiated to a degree we could never have dreamed of; all these are manufactured in scientific and business methods and delivered at our doors, or our dumb-waiters. Breakfast foods are the latest step in this direction; and the encroaching delicatessen shop with its list of allurements. Even the last and dearest stronghold, the very core and centre of domestic bliss—hot cooked food—is being served us by this irreverent professional man.

The sacred domestic rite of eating may be still performed in the sanctuary, but the once equally sacred, subsidiary art of cooking is swiftly going out of it. As to eating at home, so dear a habit, so old a habit, old enough to share with every beast that drags her prey into her lair, that she and her little ones may gnaw in safety; this remains strongly in evidence, and will for some time yet. But while it reigns unshaken in our minds let us follow, open-eyed, the great human distinction of eating together. To share one's food, to call guest and friend to the banquet, is not a custom of any animal save those close allies in social organisation, the ants and their compeers. Not only do we permit this, but it is our chiefest joy and pride. From the child playing tea-party to the Lord Mayor's Banquet, the human race shows a marked tendency to eat together. It is our one great common medium—more's the pity that we have none better as yet! To share food is the first impulse of true hospitality, the largest field of artificial extravagance. Moreover, in actual fact, in the working world, food is eaten together by almost all men at noon; and by women and men in what they call "social life" almost daily. In recent years, in our cities, this habit increases widely, swiftly; men, women, and families eat together more and more; and the eating-house increases in excellence commensurately.

Whatever our opinion of these two facts, both *are* facts—that we like to eat in " the bosom of the family " and that we equally like to eat in common. Why, then, do we so fear a change in this field? " Because of the children! " most people will reply triumphantly. Are the children, then, perfectly fed at home? Is the list of dietary diseases among our home-fed little ones a thing to boast of? May it be hinted that it is because child-feeding has remained absolutely domestic, while man-feeding has become partially civilised, that the knowledge of how to feed children is so shamefully lacking? Be all this as it may, it is plainly to be seen that our domestic conditions as to food supply are rapidly changing, and that all signs point to a steady rise in efficiency and decrease in expense in this line of human service. There remains much to be done. In no field of modern industry and business opportunity is there a wider demand to be met than in this constantly waxing demand for better food, more hygienic food, more reliable food, cheaper food, food which shall give us the maximum of nutrition and healthy pleasure, with the minimum of effort and expense. At this writing—May, 1903— there is in flourishing existence a cooked-food supply company, in New Haven (Conn.), in Pittsburgh (Pa.), and in Boston (Mass.), with doubtless others not at present known to the author.

Turning to the other great domestic industry, the care of children, we may see hopeful signs of growth. The nursemaid is improving. Those who can afford it are beginning to see that the association of a child's first years with low-class ignorance cannot be beneficial. There is a demand for " trained nurses " for children; even in rare cases the employment of some Kindergarten ability. Among the very poor the day-nursery and Kindergarten are doing slow, but beautiful work. The President of Harvard demands that more care and money be spent on the primary grades in education; and all through our school systems there is a healthy movement. Child-study is being undertaken at last. Pedagogy is being taught as a science. In our public parks there is regular provision made for children; and in the worst parts of the cities an incipient provision of playgrounds.

There is no more brilliant hope on earth to-day than this new thought about the child. In what does it consist? In recognising " the child," children as a class, children as citizens with rights to be guaranteed only by the state; instead of our previous attitude toward them of absolute personal ownership—the unchecked tyranny, or as unchecked indulgence, of the private home. Children are at last emerging from the very lowest grade of private ownership into the safe, broad level of common citizenship. That which no million separate families could give their millions of separate children, the state can give, and does. Our progress, so long merely mechanical, is at last becoming personal, touching the people and lifting them as one.

Now what is all this leading to? What have we to hope—or to dread—in the undeniable lines of development here shown? What most of us dread is this: that we shall lose our domestic privacy; that we shall lose our family dinner table; that woman will lose " her charm;" that we shall lose our children; and the child lose its mother. We are mortally afraid of separation.

THE HOME

The unfolding and differentiation of natural growth is not separation in any organic sense. The five-fingered leaf, closely bound in the bud, separates as it opens. The branches separate from the trunk as the trees grow. But this legitimate separation does not mean disconnection. The tree is as much one tree as if it grew in a strait-jacket. All growth must widen and diverge. If natural growth is checked, disease must follow. If allowed, health and beauty and happiness accompany it.

The home, if it grows on in normal lines, will not be of the same size and relative density as it was in ancient times; but it will be as truly home to the people of to-day. In trying to maintain by force the exact limits and characteristics of the primitive home, we succeed only in making a place modern man is not at home in.

The people of our time need the home of our time, not the homes of ancient barbarians. The primitive home and the home-bound woman are the continually acting causes of our increasing domestic unhappiness. By clinging to unsuitable conditions we bring about exactly the evils we are most afraid of. A little scientific imagination well based on existing facts, well in line with existing tendencies, should be used to point out the practical possibilities of the home as it is to be.

Try to consider it first with the woman out for working hours. This is an impassable gulf to the average mind. " Home, with the woman out—there is no such thing!" cries it. The instant assumption is that she will never be in, in which case I am willing to admit that there would be no home. Suppose we retrace our steps a little and approach the average mind more gradually. Can it imagine a home, a real happy home, with the woman out of it for one hour a day? Can it, encouraged by this step, picture the home as still enduring while the woman is out of it two hours a day? Is there any exact time of attendance required to make a home? What is, in truth, required to make a home? First mother and child, then father; this is the family, and the place where they live is the home.

Now the father goes out every day; does the home cease to exist because of his hours away from it? It is still his home, he still loves it, he maintains it, he lives in it, only he has a " place of business " elsewhere. At a certain stage of growth the children are out of it, between say 8.30 and 3.30. Does it cease to be home because of their hours away from it? Do they not love it and live in it—*while they are there?* Now if, while the father was out, and the children were out, the mother should also be out, would the home disappear into thin air?

THE HOME

It is home *while the family are in it.* When the family are out of it it is only a house; and a house will stand up quite solidly for some eight hours of the family's absence. Incessant occupation is not essential to a home. If the father has wife and children with him in the home when he returns to it, need it matter to him that the children are wisely cared for in schools during his absence; or that his wife is duly occupied elsewhere while they are so cared for?

Two " practical obstacles " intervene; first, the " housework "; second, the care of children below school age. The housework is fast disappearing into professional hands. When that is utterly gone, the idle woman has but one excuse—the babies. This is a very vital excuse. The baby is the founder of the home. If the good of the baby requires the persistent, unremitting care of the mother in the home, then indeed she must remain there. No other call, no other claim, no other duty, can be weighed for a moment against this all-important service —the care of the little child.

But we have already seen that if there is one thing more than another the home fails in, it is just this. If there is one duty more than another the woman fails in, it is just this. Our homes are not planned nor managed in the interests of little children; and the isolated home-

[338]

bound mother is in no way adequate to their proper rearing. This is not disputable on any side. The death rate of little children during the years they are wholly in the home and mother's care proves it beyond question. The wailing of little children who live—or before they die—wailing from bodily discomfort, nervous irritation, mental distress, punishment—a miserable sound, so common, so expected, that it affects the price of real estate, tenants not wishing to live near little children on account of their cries—this sound of world-wide anguish does not seem to prove much for the happiness of these helpless inmates of the home.

Such few data as we have of babies and young children in properly managed day nurseries, give a far higher record of health and happiness. Not the sick baby in the pauper hospital, not the lonely baby in the orphan asylum; but the baby who has *not* lost his mother, but who adds to mother's love, calm, wise, experienced professional care.

The best instance of this, as known to me, is that of M. Godin's *phalanstère* in Guise, France. An account of it can be found in the *Harper's Monthly*, November, 1885; or in M. Godin's own book, " Social Solutions," translated by Marie Howland, now out of print. This wise and successful undertaking had been going on for

over twenty years when the above article was written.
Among its features was a beautifully planned nursery
for babies and little children, and the results to child
and parent, to home and state were wholly good.   Better
health, greater peace and contentment, a swift, regular,
easy development these children enjoyed; and when, in
later years, they met the examinations of the public
schools, they stood higher than the children of any other
district in France.

A newborn baby leads a far happier, healthier, more
peaceful existence in the hands of the good trained nurse,
than it does when those skilled hands are gone, and it is
left on the trembling knees of the young, untrained
mother.

"But the nurse does not love it!" we wildly protest.
What if she does not?   Cannot the mother love it *while
the nurse takes care of it?*   This is the whole position in
a nutshell.   Nothing is going to prevent the mother from
loving her children in one deep, ceaseless river of calm
affection, with such maternal transports as may arise
from time to time in addition; but nothing ought to
prevent the child's being properly taken care of while
the love is going on.   The mother is not ashamed to
depend on the doctor if the child is ill, on the specialist
if the child is defective, on the teacher when the child is

in school. Why should she so passionately refuse to depend on equally skilled assistance for the first five years of her babies' lives—those years when iron statistics remorselessly expose her incapacity?

The home that is coming will not try to be a workshop, a nursery, or a school. The child that is coming will find a more comfortable home than he ever had before, and something else besides—a place for babies to be happy in, and grow up in, without shrieks of pain. The mother that is coming, a much more intelligent person than she has ever been before, will recognise that this ceaseless procession of little ones requires some practical provision for its best development, other than what is possible in the passing invasion of the home. " How a baby does tyrannise over the household! " we complain, vaguely recognising that the good of the baby requires something different from the natural home habits of adults. We shall finally learn to make a home for the babies too.

This involves great changes in both our idea of home, and our material provision for it. Why not? Growth is change, and there is need of growth here. Slowly, gradually, by successive experiments, we shall find out how to meet new demands; and these experiments are now being made, in all the living centres of population.

XVII

RESULTS

TO us, who have for so many unbroken generations been wholly bound to the home, who honestly believe that its service and maintenance constitute the whole duty of men and women, the picture of a world in which home and its affairs takes but a small part of life's attention gives rather a blank outlook. What else are we to do! What else to love—what else to serve eternally! What else to revere, to worship! How shall we occupy the hands of man if but a tithe of his labour supports him in comfort; how fill the heart of woman, when her family are happily and rightly served without sacrificing her in the operation! It is hard, at first—we being so accustomed to spend all life in merely keeping ourselves alive—to see what life might be when we had some to spare. We find it difficult to imagine this "world of trouble" as rid of its troubles; as rationally and comfortably managed; peaceful, clean, safe, healthy, giving everyone room and time to grow. Nor need we labour to forecast events too accurately; especially the material details which must be decided by long experiment. No rigid prescription is needed; no dictum as to whether we shall live in small separate houses, greenly gardened, with closely connected conveniences for service and for education, for work and play; or in towering palaces with shaded flower-bright courts and cloisters. All that must work out as have our great modern wonders in other lines, little by little, in orderly development. But what we can forecast in safety is the effect on the human body and the human soul.

A peaceful, healthy, happy babyhood and childhood, with such delicate adjustment of educational processes as we already see indicated, will give us a far better individual. The full-grown mother, contributing racial advance in both body and mind, will add greatly to this gain. We can be better people everywhere, better born, bred, fed, educated in all ways. But quite beyond this is the rich growth of our long aborted social instincts, which will rapidly follow the reduction of these long artificially maintained primitive and animal instincts.

Where now trying to meet general needs by personal efforts, modern needs by ancient methods, we must perforce manifest an intense degree of self-interest to keep up the struggle; as soon as we meet these needs easily, swiftly, inexpensively, by modern methods and common efforts, less self-interest will be necessary.

When sidewalks were narrow and streets foul, great was the jostling, keen the resentment—" You take the wall of me, sir!" Where all is broad, clean, safe, no such hot feeling exists. We do not truly prefer to be always sharply looking out for ourselves; it is much more interesting to look out for each other; but this method of handicapping each man with his own affiairs, in such needless weight, keeps up a selfishness which true civilisation tends steadily to eliminate. Social instincts in social conditions are as natural as animal instincts in animal conditions.

Starving, shipwrecked sailors, robbed of all social advantages, are reduced sometimes even to cannibalism. Polite people at a banquet show no hint of such fierce, relentless greed. Relieved of the necessity for spending our whole time taking care of ourselves, we shall deliciously launch forward into the much larger pleasure of taking care of one another. Relieved of the ceaseless, instant pressure of purely physical needs, we shall be able to put forth the true demands of human life at last. The mind, no longer penned in its weary treadmill of private affairs, will spread into its legitimate area—public affairs. We shall be able to see a greater number of things at once, and care about them. That larger-mindedness will be an immediate result; for we have already far more capacity than we use.

We have developed the modern civilised mind, the social mind, through the world's work; but we bury it, enslave it, stultify it, in the home's work. A new power —a new sense of range—freedom, growth, as of a great stream flowing freely; plenty of force to work with, plenty of room to work in—this is what will follow as we learn to properly relate the home to the rest of life.

Once the mind rises, free, outside those old enclosing, crushing walls, it will see life with different eyes. Our common good will appear to us as naturally as our private good does now. At present the average mind does not seem able to grasp a great general fact, be it for good or evil.

To make a man appreciate the proposed advantage, realise the impending or existing evil, we must " bring it home to him," make him feel it " where he lives." When his home does not occupy most of his mind, tax his strength, reduce his range of interest and affection, he can see the big things more easily. When he " lives " in the whole city—i. e., thinks about it, cares about it, works for it, loves it—then he will promptly feel anything that affects it in any part. This common love and

[345]

care are just as possible to human beings as love and care for one's own young are possible to the beasts. It is possible; it is natural; it is a great and increasing joy; but its development is checked by a system which requires all our love and care for our own, and even then does not properly provide for them.

The love of human beings for each other is not a dream of religion, it is a law of nature. It is bred of human contact, of human relation, of human service; it rests on identical interest and the demands of a social development which must include all, if it permanently lift any. Against this perfectly natural development stands this opposing shell; this earlier form of life, essential in its place, most mischievous out of it; this early cradle of humanity in which lie smothered the full-grown people of to-day.

Must we then leave it—lose it—go without it? Never. The more broadly socialised we become, the more we need our homes to rest in. The large area is necessary for the human soul; the big, modern, civilised social nature. But we are still separate animal beings as well as collective social beings. Always we need to return to the dear old ties, to the great primal basis, that we may rise refreshed and strengthened, like Antæus from the earth. Private, secluded, sweet, wholly our own; not invaded by any trade or work or business, not open to the crowd; the place of the one initial and undying group of father, mother, and child, will remain to us. These, and the real friend, are all that belong to the home.

It should be the recognised base and background of our lives; but those lives must be lived in their true area, the world. And so lived, by both of us, all of us; shared in by the child, served in by the woman as well as the man; that world will grow to have the sense of intimacy, of permanent close attachment, of comfort and pleasure and rest, which now attaches only to the home.

So, living, really living in the world and loving it, the presence there of father, mother, and child will gradually bring out in it all the beauty and safety, the refreshment and strength we so vainly seek to ensure in our private home. The sense of duty, of reverence, of love, honestly transferred to the world we live in, will have its natural, its inevitable effect, and make that world our home at last.

THE END